BRITAIN IN OLD PHOTOGRAPHS

LOWESTOFT
WITHIN LIVING MEMORY

IAN G. ROBB

Ken Carsey at Richards Ironworks Shipyard on the South Quay, seen here in a portrait taken in about 1980 in Richards' Steelwork Department. As a keen photographer he recorded launches at the Richards Shipyard as well as the changing town in which he lived. Many of his photographs appear in this book and are being published for the first time. *(Ken Carsey)*

First published 2012

The History Press
The Mill, Brimscombe Port
Stroud, Gloucestershire, GL5 2QG
www.thehistorypress.co.uk

© Ian G. Robb, 2012

The right of Ian G. Robb to be identified as the Author of this work has been asserted in accordance with the Copyrights, Designs and Patents Act 1988.

All rights reserved. No part of this book may be reprinted or reproduced or utilised in any form or by any electronic, mechanical or other means, now known or hereafter invented, including photocopying and recording, or in any information storage or retrieval system, without the permission in writing from the Publishers.
British Library Cataloguing in Publication Data.
A catalogue record for this book is available from the British Library.

ISBN 978 0 7524 6278 3

Typesetting and origination by The History Press
Printed in Great Britain

CONTENTS

	Introduction	5
1	Post-war Reconstruction	7
2	The 1960s & '70s	23
3	The 1980s: The beginning of the end	45
4	The 1990s: The End of an Era	77
5	The Millennium & Beyond	107
	Acknowledgements	128

The Eagle Brewery, Whapload Road, late 1950s. This austere barrack-like brewery was located between Rants Score and Martin Score. It was originally built for Youngman & Preston in the nineteenth century. After the Second World War it became Divers & Son, surviving into the 1960s as part of Charringtons when it was demolished to make way for extensions to the Birds Eye factory. Seen here is the main entrance, over which were two stone eagles. During the subsequent demolition only one of the eagles was saved and at one time adorned the Birds Eye offices in Whapload Road.

INTRODUCTION

In this, the Diamond Jubilee year of HM Queen Elizabeth II, Lowestoft stands at a crossroads. Life in the town is very different compared with that of sixty years ago. Many of us who were born not long after the Second World War recall that as late as 1977 and the Queen's Silver Jubilee, Lowestoft seemed to have a bright future in its established industries of fishing, shipbuilding, food production, coachbuilding and manufacturing. However, by 2002 and the Queen's Golden Jubilee, things were rapidly changing.

For those of us now reaching their mid-sixties and born as part of the post-war baby-boom, we have seen Lowestoft alter beyond recognition over the past six decades. The loss of friends and colleagues in recent years have made me realise that memory is ephemeral. What was once ordinary everyday life, like pre-decimal coinage or working on the Fish Market, has become part of history, and part of the town's heritage.

In 1946, when many of the first of the town's baby-boomers were born, they spent their early years in the midst of the reconstruction of a port which had played an important part in the Second World War. In 1952, we all became New Elizabethans. For us young children now at school, the new queen became synonymous with the changes that were occurring all around us; green spaces to play on, newly built schools, free milk, and finally on reaching school leaving age, a chance to work alongside uncle, dad or granddad as an apprentice at such prestigious firms as Eastern Coachworks, Brooke Marine or Richards Ironworks. For the more adventurous, many chose fishing. Always a risky trade and therefore highly respected, it was a profession that nevertheless worried many a family, especially those steeped in a seafaring tradition. In my case, in 1962 when I considered 'the boats', I was placed by concerned parents in the office at Explorator, albeit part of Small & Co., then the largest fishing fleet in the port. My father knew several people at Small's and they made sure I never went on any of their boats – an office on the Fish Market was the closest I ever got! Their concerns were genuine, of course; as late as the mid-1960s, Lowestoft boats were still disappearing in the North Sea – either blown up by rogue Second World War mines or caught in inclement weather for the North Sea was no forgiving mistress!

The fishing industry with its smokehouses, fish houses and net stores, was the largest employer in Lowestoft. The port was in a strong position, surviving the loss of the centuries-old North Sea herring fishery in 1966, an event that saw the end of Great Yarmouth as a fishing port. Lowestoft was able to turn from drifters to trawlers and continued fishing for another twenty years.

Despite the extensive destruction during the war, much of Lowestoft's medieval and Tudor heritage survived, as did the Beach community. Whereas the Beach was effectively abandoned after the 1953 flood, those ancient buildings in the old town on the cliff that had survived the war – the Old Market Place, Mariners Street, White Horse Street, Dove Street, Duke's Head Street, Crown Street, Chapel Street, the old Gun Lane and the Hemplands among them – succumbed to the bulldozer from the late 1950s to the mid-1960s. This included remnants of the old China Factory. Of these ancient buildings, hardly anything was recorded for posterity. In 1968, Lowestoft's only high-rise, St Peter's Court, was built on part of the site.

If the years from the 1950s to the late 1970s were generally an era of improvement, the decades following witnessed the reverse. The 1980s saw several notable closures with Brooke Marine, Eastern Coachworks and Morton's among the largest. The 1990s saw even more closures with the ending of the CWS factory and Lowestoft Canning. Richards Ironworks, a century-old shipbuilder, was to be followed by the unspeakable – the decline of Lowestoft's fishing fleet. Kirkley, once the wealthiest suburb of Lowestoft, rapidly became one of the poorest. The last of Lowestoft's fishing fleet left the port in 2002, the same year we celebrated HM Queen Elizabeth II's Golden Jubilee.

Strolling along today's South Quay promenade from the Bascule Bridge to Riverside Road and on to the outskirts of Oulton Broad, it is almost impossible to believe that only twenty years ago that same stretch of quayside echoed to the sound of boats being built and the chatter of men and women packing frozen or tinned foods. In total there were some 15,000 men and women, part-time and full-time, involved in food production, shipbuilding, timber yards and television manufacturing. Today, this once-busy harbour rings to the gentle sound of yachts sailing to and from Oulton Broad, and where Richards and Morton's once were, we observe cars heading into the Asda supermarket car park.

Renewable industries, oil and gas rigs construction are now Lowestoft's main industries. The resort is still with us, however, but is now concentrated mainly around the South Beach and Esplanade instead of involving the whole town.

One thing that remains unchanged is the Bridge. While Great Yarmouth, only 10 miles up the road, had their four-lane road bridge in 1929, when it came to Lowestoft and the need for a new bridge in 1969 (after its Victorian Jubilee Swing Bridge finally packed up after 72 years of service), hopes for a bridge to rival its Norfolk neighbour as well as a start on its own third crossing were in vain, alas, and the phrase 'Bridger' remains synonymous to the increasing queues of traffic on both sides of today's Bridge.

I hope that this book will bring back memories of a time not so long ago; in many cases, it seems only yesterday. To those younger New Elizabethans, who ask their grandparents 'what was it like when you were young?' I hope this book will go some way to show how great Lowestoft once was.

1

POST-WAR RECONSTRUCTION

Leaving-off time, Eastern Coachworks, mid-1950s. Until the mid-1960s almost everyone cycled to work. Although the town had revived enough of its pre-war industries to retain its position as an important manufacturing centre as well as a fishing port, most people cycled, or rode a moped to work – one of which here dates the photo to approximately 1956. According to the late Jack Rose the men are coming out of Eastern Coachworks.

Above: London Road North, 1949. The town centre still retained a wartime feel about it. Bonsalls and T. Gore's (left, nearest the camera) both moved here after the Waller Raid of January 1942. Boarded-up upper storeys indicate the Lowestoft Co-op – tin baths and electric coppers were displayed under the shelter. One of the earliest childhood memories I have is of looking into the Co-op window! Matthes Bakery sticks out onto the pavement. Damage from the Waller Raid is still evident on the upper floors of shops further up London Road North.

Left: The Candy Shop, 25 High Street, May 1949. The shop had been wrecked in the Fokker-Wulf raid of 1943, revealing its earlier fabric. An open doorway on the first floor confirms that nos 24 (demolished) and 25 were once one large building. Bomb-sites were a popular way to advertise forthcoming attractions: *Cheyenne* was showing at the Palace that week followed by *Spring in Park Lane*.

Number one (Yarmouth Road) housing estate, Gunton, 1949. Looking across from Hollingsworth Road to Harris Avenue, Minos Road and Mylodon Road, this was the first housing estate built after the war. The roads were laid out by young German prisoners of war in late 1945, but shortages of men and materials meant the estate took over four years to complete. The fencing on the right belonged to Ashley Downs Boys' Home.

Railway carriages, Kirkley Run, late 1940s. Lowestoft suffered an acute housing shortage in the years after the war. When the military left the area many families desperate for accommodation occupied the abandoned camps at Pakefield and Oulton. Others turned railway carriages and wooden sheds into homes such as these in the Kirkley Run area, which were still in use in the early 1950s.

August Bank Holiday, Gunton Denes, 1950. The beaches were now comparatively mine-free which meant that people in north Lowestoft returned to sunbathe on what, if I recall, used to be known as 'Our Beach' to define it from the South Beach resort on the other side of the Bridge, then given over to the visitor trade. Generally known as the North Beach, family days out were becoming popular, although many parents tended to walk the mile or so to Gunton Denes pushing a pram with older toddlers walking beside them. Once there, two-year-old Forbes attempts to avoid being covered by his older brother Ian's endeavour at building a sandcastle. Mother Gladys Robb sits with the family pet – the aptly named Doggie – while in the background campers have pitched their tents for the day, sheltering themselves from the breeze behind sand dunes and clumps of marram grass. The camera Mr R. was using was a pre-war Rolleicord, a souvenir of his time in the army during the war!

Yarmouth Road, looking towards Lowestoft North railway station, leading towards Gunton, c. 1954. Although a post-war scene, very little had changed since the days just before the war. The bushes on the corner of Sussex Road (left) hide nearby allotments, while the police phone box indicated the entrance. The view was taken at what older folk of the time knew as the town boundary; apart from the pre-war lamp posts, there is also the obvious lack of footpath on the left-hand side of Yarmouth Road. This changed once you crossed over the railway bridge (behind the Austin car) reaching Lowestoft Secondary Grammar School, recognisable in the distance on the left by its roof and turrets. Vehicles were fewer in number, which explains why some of the pedestrians tended to walk on the road instead of using the pavement. Between the car and the cyclist travelling towards the camera is the entrance to Station Road. Behind the cyclist are the advertising hoardings outside Lowestoft North station on the Great Yarmouth to Lowestoft line. The anonymous photographer would take his or her life in their hands today to achieve such a view!

Above: South Pier and Yacht Basin, before 1954. The Victorian Pier pavilion was in a sorry state following the war, and much of the damage had been caused not only by enemy action but by Royal Naval personnel. The state of the Yacht Basin side of the pavilion, however, was the result of a direct hit destroying the bandstand and part of the pier. The pavilion was demolished in 1954 to make way for a new South Pier Pavilion and tower which opened in 1956.

Left: Festival of Britain design for brochure, 1951. This was a piece of artwork by a student of Lowestoft School of Art probably as part of a competition held by the borough for its own part in the festival. The official logo was designed by the famous Abram Games; this particular design was rejected, I suspect, because the borough coat of arms was superimposed on the festival logo itself. *(Paul Allison)*

Above: Anguish Street and East Street. On the night of 31 January/1 February, 1953, the east coast of England suffered its most severe flooding since November 1897. The Beach community was devastated and all but abandoned. In September 1964 it was decided to demolish the whole area. Anguish Street and East Street are seen here in 1967, not long before demolition. Fish-houses and yards still worked up to the end. *(Ken Carsey)*

Right: Lowestoft Flood Relief Fund Concert programme, 19 February 1953. Nearly three weeks later the Hippodrome Theatre was able to hold a special concert to help those affected by the flood. Many on the bill were serious amateurs helping to do their bit: tenor Roy Pashley, and soprano Monica Durrant, for example, who were joined by Miss Tova Larsen from the Royal Danish Academy of Music and the Suffolk comedian, Tommy Crawford.

Coronation street party, Monckton Avenue, June 1953. Children of all ages celebrate with their parents and grandparents the crowning of the young Queen Elizabeth II. Many children here were first generation baby-boomers even though several look as though they were born during the war itself. Although it had finished nearly eight years before, the war's aftermath meant that some rationing still affected daily life. Regardless of the shortages though, everyone made sure the children had a thoroughly good time commemorating the crowning of the new monarch. Several of the houses display photos of the new queen and the tablecloth – a length of paper with red, white and blue strips (usually with a crown and EIIR) – would be repeated on trestle tables across the town. Trifles, sandwiches and cake washed down with lemonade were the order of the day. This would be followed later by the purchase of a Coronation mug or cup and saucer – and, of course, the obligatory commemorative school photograph. It was from this day, Tuesday 2 June 1953, that we all officially became New Elizabethans – children of a brave new era. *(Ernest Graystone)*

Opposite: Bridge Road, late 1950s. Looking towards Victoria Road junction (on the right), the light coloured shop on the corner was Reginald Elliott's newsagents, later remembered as L. & R. Taylor's. Taylor's also had a branch in the town centre. The tin building on the right appears to have been a congregational church. There is still an aspect of the countryside, especially on the left, but things were changing. Note the new street lights.

Lowestoft drifters, Waveney Dock, *c.* 1954. Nearest the camera is LT137 *Norfolk Yeoman* followed by LT7 *Shepherd Lad* a pre-war drifter, and LT387 *Young Duke*. In 1949 Small & Co. had been one of the first to rebuild their fishing fleet, of which two are seen here. The Scots had returned as did the Prunier Trophy and for a while it appeared that the herring fishery would return to something like its pre-war strength.

London Road North, c. 1954. Then about to be reconstructed after the carnage of the Second World War; in 1946 this was to be the site of Lowestoft's new Civic Centre. From Regent Road (on the extreme left) to Milton Road, beyond the Journal office on the right, it was planned to be a smaller but just as grand version of Norwich City Hall. Plans were drawn up and an artist's impression appeared on the front page of the *Lowestoft Journal*. Then disaster – in December 1946 the Sea Wall, already in a perilous state, collapsed and all the money earmarked for the Civic Centre went on constructing a new North Denes sea defence on the landward side of the previous wall. It was then suggested that the London Road North bomb-site should temporarily become an estate of prefabs to alleviate the town's acute housing shortage. At the time of the photograph, much of the site was up for sale with only Walker's Stores, Lowestoft Journal, Eastern Daily Press and Morlings returning to their old addresses. The tall television aerial on the horizon in the centre of the photograph may belong to Morlings who were demonstrating the new medium of television, albeit then with only one available channel. A new building, possibly a florist's, stands beside Walker's and the older Journal office. In the street, fashions appear to cover a mixed period from hints of wartime utility to the latest fashion. Cars were nowhere to be seen, everyone walking, travelling by bus, or, as here, cycling. Regretfully, we never did get our Civic Centre.

Opposite, top: Prince Philip, Duke of Edinburgh, reviewing troops in Denmark Road outside Lowestoft Central station, May 1956. He had arrived by train to open the new South Pier Pavilion. The town turned out to see the duke as he also visited some of the Boston Deep Sea fishing boats moored at the Trawl Dock. This had not been the first time he had visited Lowestoft; as Prince Philip of Greece he was here as a seven-year-old boy in the 1920s.

Opposite, bottom: Ancient houses, Mariners Street, looking west towards Church Road, 1950s. The Hemplands, the town's ancient rope-making area, is between the Morning Star and the old merchant house converted many decades before into three smaller dwellings; its large central chimney suggests early Tudor. If I recall (I was very young at the time), the wall on the corner facing the side of the Morning Star was mainly constructed of flint.

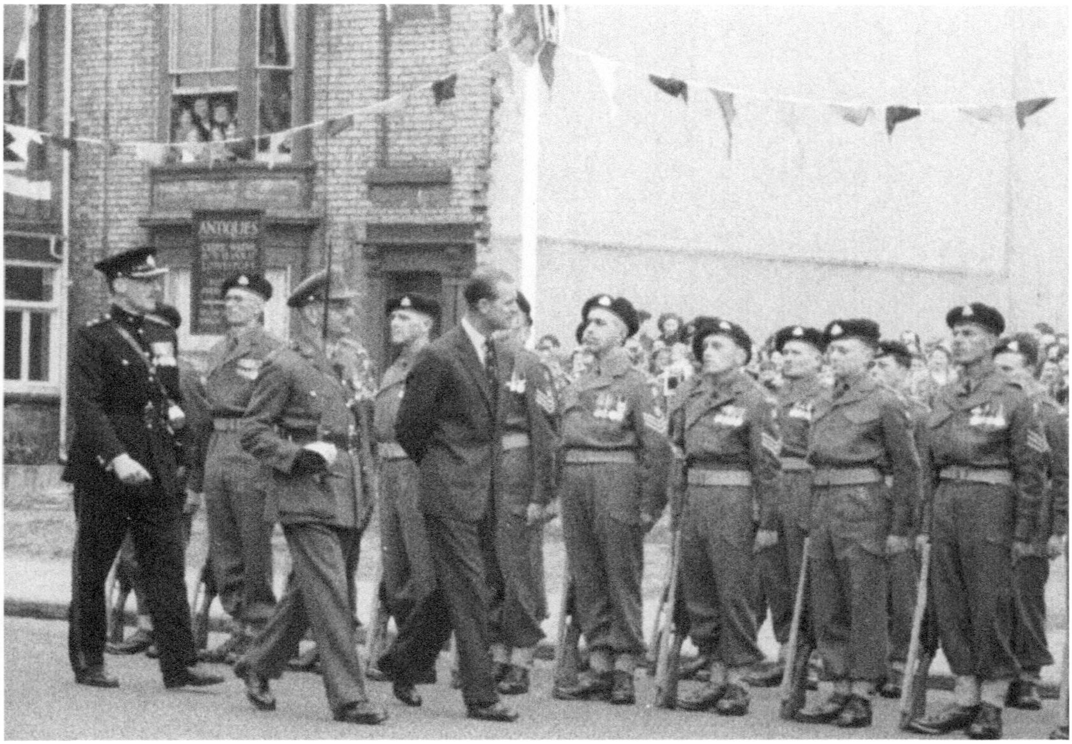
ANTIQUES

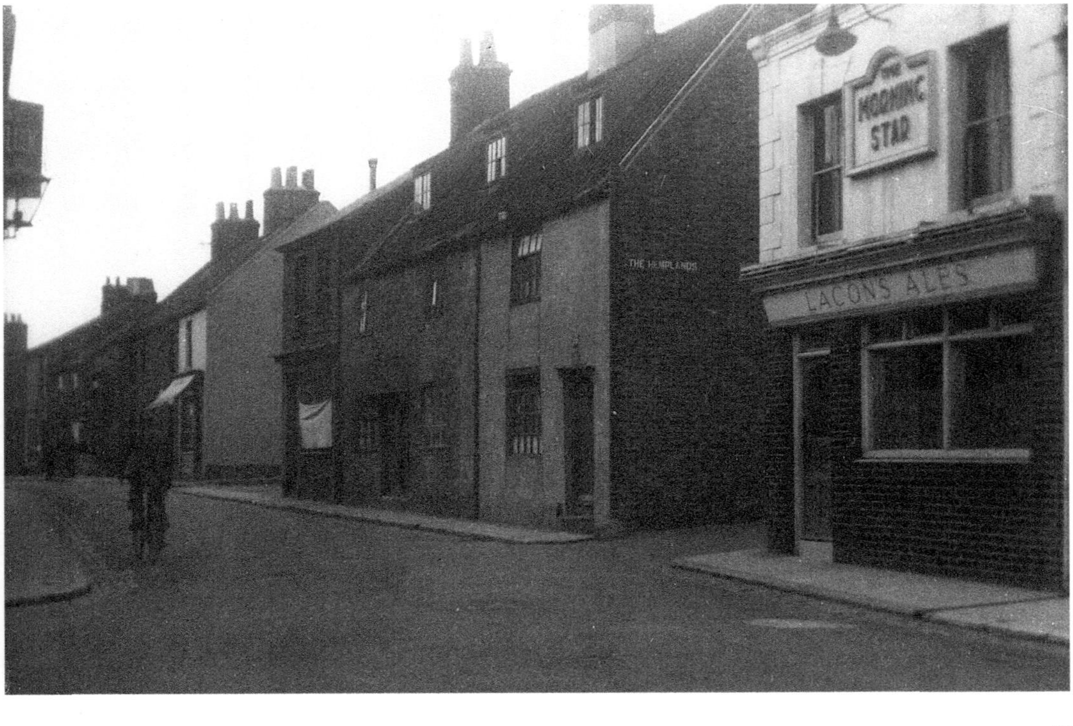
THE
MORNING
STAR
THE HEMPLANDS
LACONS ALES

Lawrence Green, gents' outfitters, High Street. In the late 1950s and into the early 1960s, young Lowestoft fishermen had their own version of a 'going ashore' suit; wide trouser legs, individually cut jackets and waistcoat – the whole ensemble was made to order. Most of the young lads preferred gaudy colours including pink and lavender. Many of these suits were made by Lawrence Green, whose shop is seen here in 1993. *(Author)*

LT295 *Suffolk Maid* was a diesel drifter trawler built by Richards for Small & Co. and launched in 1957. In their day the young crewmen standing on the bow of the vessel may have been some of Lawrence Green's customers. In the late 1950s and the years leading up to 1963 Richards built mainly fishing vessels; for post-war Lowestoft the 1950s were the pinnacle of the North Sea herring fishing. *(Ernest Graystone)*

Eastern Counties buses arriving outside Lowestoft Central railway station, *c.* 1960. Tuttles department store is on the corner of Waveney Road and London Road North. The two buses seen here were Bristol Lodekkas with bodies built in Lowestoft; the one on the right is on the Oulton Broad circuit. The misty silhouette between the 20A bus and Tuttles is the South Pier pavilion. The van is a Morris Commercial. Note the scooter riders with no crash helmets! *(Kenny Harper)*

Commer van and trailer, *c.* 1955. For many years Matthes Bakery produced the best-known brand of sliced bread in East Anglia – Sunshine Bread. Based in Gorleston, they had three shops in the town as well as a bakery in Oxford Road. Although P.W. Watson's coachbuilding heyday was before the war, they continued to build some very impressive vehicles into the 1950s as this high-capacity 15ft 9in wheelbase bread van proves.

The Prince Albert public house on the corner of Park Road, 1950s. This is the original pub seen from Melbourne Road. An Adnams house, the painted sign on the side announces all beers were drawn from the wood. George Youngs was mine host at this time. At the end of Melbourne Road, on the extreme right, is the Hemplands. The old pub was rebuilt in the 1960s to a design by Tayler and Green, Lowestoft architects with a national reputation. *(RPA/the late Jack Rose)*

London Road North, late 1950s. Looking north from Beach Road towards the Odeon cinema. Of particular interest here is the group of uniformed schoolchildren walking past Foster & Co. and Currys towards the junction of Surrey Street without any noticeable chaperon. Of the shops; on the left is the blind from Purdy's the bakers, which, if I recall, had a café on the first floor. Foster & Co. were wine and spirit merchants, while Currys mainly dealt in bicycles – a far cry from today's Currys megastore on the North Quay retail park. Bonsalls, Gore's and the old Co-op store had all gone to make way for the present terrace of shops. Barclay's Bank moved here from Commercial Road in 1964, later followed by Lipton's and the Eastern Gas showrooms. Behind the recently erected lamp post, Matthes' new single-storey shop stands in line with the rest of the street. A lone cyclist passes a parked Jaguar. Although there appears to be traffic further up the street, the fact was that you could park in the town centre to do your shopping! Between Matthes and Timothy Whites is an alleyway leading to Day's Garage in Clapham Road. The Odeon survived the war to become one of the two town centre Saturday junior cinema clubs, which brings me back to the group of schoolchildren. The image is not clear enough to clarify their school. With their coats over their arms, satchels, bags and books, were they making their way to the railway station?

Opposite: The Rising Sun, Whapload Road, 1960s. Fondly remembered as the fishermen's pub; it was nicknamed the 'Japanese Embassy'. In its time it was famous as the venue for one of the first outside live BBC TV broadcasts *Saturday Night Out* in February 1956 which was also the first live TV broadcast from Lowestoft. 'Bloater' Nicholson was mine host until 1966. Reg Reynolds, its last landlord, pulled the final pint in November 1968. *(The late Jack Rose)*

Lowestoft Swing Bridge, 1959, taken from the top of a double-decker bus, looking from the south side towards Waveney Road and the turret of Tuttles department store. Officially called the Jubilee Bridge, it was opened in 1897 to replace the much narrower swing bridge that had been built in 1830. At the time of the photograph, this was also the major trunk route from Great Yarmouth to London. Until the coming of the railway to Lowestoft in 1847, the bulk of Lowestoft's traffic travelled via the North Sea and Oulton Broad, hence the narrowness of the first two structures. The railway was the town's first reliable land route but with its subsequent decline, it became obvious as early as 1954 that the town needed a much larger and wider crossing as well as a third crossing elsewhere in the borough to deal with the increasing volume of road traffic. In fact, by the 1960s if you turned up late for work, especially on the Fish Market, the Bridge always got the blame! Kirkley suffered the most, however, with traffic queues as far back as Pakefield. The house on the right was one of two built for the original bridge, its companion on the north side disappeared with the construction of the bridge shown here. The turret on the corner belonged to Tuttles department store's furniture department; it was destroyed by fire in July 1964. Near the camera is Craske's fuel merchant, a subsidiary of Small & Co. Like many of the larger fishing businesses in Lowestoft, Small's had interests connected in one way or another with fishing. Note the two semaphores: one, I think, was of metal and the other a red flag. These were raised or lowered to indicate when the bridge was open or shut.

2

THE 1960s & '70s

The maiden voyage of LT395 *Suffolk Punch*, 1961. She was built by Richards Ironworks, a shipbuilder whose designers gave Lowestoft fishing vessels a unique style. Sold in October 1974 to Putford Enterprises, she was renamed the *Hatherleigh*. In 1983 she was then converted to standby duties and left Lowestoft in 1992. *(Ernest Graystone)*

London Road North, *c.* 1960. Taken during the summer season, the group on the left is window shopping at Timothy Whites, once a chemist, but in its latter days mainly dealing in hardware. Frying pans would cost you 7*s* 6*d*; buckets shown in the window were priced at 6*s* 11*d* and obviously not of the bucket and spade seaside variety! Overy's the tobacconists and hairdresser had opened before the First World War and were still there in 1960 – or at least the shop was. As a small boy I recall my parents buying sweets there. Later on in the decade it became a branch of Coopers, selling decorative glass and chinaware. Fielding's cycles, radio and television dealers were eventually taken over by Halfords. Johnsons the dyers shared their shop with a hairdresser; Messon's confectioners is followed by Craiks, and then the Odeon cinema showing *Peyton Place*. Beyond the Odeon were Paige's, British Home Stores, and a plethora of businesses including Woolworths. What is noticeable in this scene are the two distinct tonal differences in the pavement. The darker tone defines where the gardens were before 1922; the original footpath is on the right. Shops were still allowed to display their goods and hoardings (as seen here on the right near the Odeon).

Right: H.T. Pye, pork butchers, 87 High Street, c. 1960. In the nineteenth century this shop was known as the Exhibition Stores, one of Lowestoft's many public houses. It has been a butcher for many years. In the 1950s no. 88 (on the right) was G. & P. James' hairdressers. The street pavement levels have changed over recent decades, rising to doorstep level in the 1990s to the detriment of no. 88, which, like many premises in the area, one has to step down into the shop.

Below: Gunn & Hill, London Road North, November, 1962. A great stock clearance sale offers 4*d* in the shilling off all prices including the wallpapers displayed in the window. Today the shop has changed little compared with the Fox and Hounds public house on the right. The house behind is in Old Nelson Street. The Adelaide – on the left – is still with us today as the Welcome.

LT182 *Tobago*, March 1964. The trawler was returning with what was reported to be one of its best catches of the season when she was driven ashore onto the North Extension as she was coming into port. Unable to land its catch, the *Tobago* remained stranded for several weeks before she could be moved. In the meantime the fish below began to decompose. Needless to say, the smell hung over the town for some time! *(Val Allison)*

Icing boxes of fish ready for loading, late 1950s. Like many of my generation, I went straight into work, into jobs prepared by the family. In my case it was into the Battery Green Road offices of Explorator. Their packing station was on the ground floor with sales offices on the first. Lorries were loaded at the old Trawl Market opposite. There, the boxes of fish were packed into insulated container lorries ready for overnight delivery anywhere between Wokingham, Rugby, London and Milford Haven. The container on the left has runners along the interior which would take metal boxes usually with up to 4st of fish (herrings or other whole fish) in them. Fillets were always packed in wooden boxes. The boxes had been brought across from Battery Green Road by jalopy, the name given to a three-wheeler single-cylinder Lister. I believe Explorator had about two or three of these to transport fish around and about the Fish Market. Their brakes were basic and led to more than one accident when one of these fully laden machines would attempt to slide on the fish slime towards the dock. I recall only one actually falling into the dock, however, taking its driver with it. Fortunately, the man survived. One of the last of these jalopies was owned by J.T. Cole in the 1970s.

Opposite: LT310 *WFP* (named after W. Frank Podd) seen here leaving the Trawl Basin, *c.* 1962. She was built by Richards as a diesel drifter-trawler in 1950 (not at Fraserburgh, as I once believed) and was powered by a specially designed 300hp AKD diesel engine. Peeping over the wheelhouse is the Royal Hotel, demolished in 1973. The spire of St John's is to the right.

Borough gardeners, High Lighthouse, High Street, 1963. While Lowestoft was a borough, it maintained an army of nurserymen who looked after the town's flowerbeds, parks and grass areas, keeping the resort looking its best for visitors. I can't quite make out the year's motif, but there is a model windmill as part of the decoration. To the left is the historic High Light. Inside this building are the remains of the first lighthouse, built in 1676.

Corporation bus terminus, London Road, Pakefield, 1963. A 1947 AEC Regent with an Eastern Coachworks body waits to return to north Lowestoft at the same stop trams once used until their withdrawal in 1931. The only memento left is the Tramways Hotel on the right. Looking north beyond the hotel, we see the petrol station at the junction of Pakefield Street. The small terrace of shops on the left date back to the late eighteenth century.

Right: Greaves' bakery, nos 67 and 69 St Peter's Street, *c.* 1964. Printed from a badly preserved negative, Charles Henry Greaves took over the business of William Utting who had been a baker on the corner with Tennyson Road in the 1920s. It appears that Mr Greaves also ran an off-licence on the premises; Morgans were a brewery based in Norwich. The shop and the houses on the left were demolished at the end of the 1960s to make way for a car park.

Below: Oulton Broad, 1963. Viewed from Bridge Road and looking across towards Swonnell's Maltings on the opposite shore in Caldecott Road, in the foreground is the pre-war remnant of Bridge Road as it was left in 1939 and the opening of the then new bridge over Mutford Lock. The war stopped any further development and it always seemed strange to me that it survived into the 1990s basically as we see it here.

These Victorian East Anglian Ice Company offices in Riverside Road were earmarked for demolition in 1964 when it was finally decided that Lowestoft should have its second road crossing. As the Ice Company was part of Small's, I recall as a young and very junior clerk, coming down here to help clear out some of the old buildings. Seen here sixteen years later in May 1980, we were still waiting for that bridge. *(Ken Carsey)*

Nearly thirty years on and derelict, the old Riverside Road East Anglian Ice Company offices were still with us in 2008, much to my surprise! Everything else around it had altered beyond recognition. It was finally demolished in 2010. The much-needed bridge never materialised despite both sides of Lake Lothing being cleared. *(Author)*

F.P. Newson's Boatyard, Commodore Road, Oulton Broad, 1965. On the back of the photograph is written 'Best Wishes/Dave & Amy'; could this be Dave standing on the stern of *Topaz?* Newson was one of many small boatyards to be found along the shores of Oulton Broad. Commodore Road had three other boatbuilding yards; Little Boats, Waveney Cruisers and Darby's.

This small racing car in Gunton's School of Motoring's window in Bevan Street (now Bevan Street East) always intrigued me, particularly in 1964 when I went there to learn to drive. The machine was the real thing, raced before the war by Mr Gunton's father. Apart from the road signs, this 1970s window display looked little different to that in the mid-1960s, when I learnt to drive in a late 1950s three-speed Ford Anglia! *(Ken Carsey)*

Rants Score, looking east towards the Gasworks from the High Street down towards the Beach village, c. 1968. Rants Score is the only score in the old town wide enough for wheeled vehicles and faces Duke's Head Street opposite on the landward side. The Beach community never fully recovered from the 1953 flood; by 1968 much of the old community had been demolished. The houses on the right went in the early 1970s. *(Author)*

Days Garage and showrooms became one of many to take advantage of the new Beach development. Photographed in Whapload Road in the early 1970s, this subsidiary of Small & Co. moved from its cramped quarters in Clapham Road to a much more spacious location not far from the Fish Market. Although in an area which continued to be a flood plain – as does all of Whapload Road to this day – no flooding has occurred since apart from one close call within the last decade. They were quite confident in the industry's future to be this close to the market. Many fish companies still had yards nearby, so a display of both good second-hand lorries and the latest in vans – note the new and as yet to be registered Ford Transits – was obviously what was needed. Looking at the three second-hand vehicles on the right, of the two versions of the Thames Trader, the one on the left next to the Transit, ABJ221B, is a 1964 snub-nosed version, and I seem to recall a similar lorry as part of the Explorator fleet. I'm not too sure of the one in the middle of the three lorries – Explorator also had versions of this long-nose version; but then so did almost all of Small & Co.'s fleets. The lorry on the extreme right, the most recent of the three, had a unique and somewhat unnerving cab-tilting mechanism to get to the engine. Rossfish had several of these vehicles while at Lowestoft. The photographer did not mention what the plume of smoke was in the background; I assume it belonged to one of the demolition teams then working on what remained of the old Beach village. *(Ernest Graystone)*

Opposite: The old Coastguard Station, Newcombe Road, seen here in 1969 amid the wholesale demolition then taking place in the area. Ancient fish houses, smokehouses and old boatsheds – some dating back to the eighteenth century – were being pulled down to be turned into the present North Denes industrial area. Many of the old street names disappeared; some – like Newcombe Road – were given to new roads close by. Old Nelson Street is in the upper left background.

In January 1969 Lowestoft's Swing Bridge got stuck in the 'open' position, effectively cutting the town in half. I was on my way to the Fish Market when it happened. There had been warning signs that the old Bridge, then nearly seventy-two years old, was in urgent need of replacement. The paddle boat *Norwich Belle* acted as a temporary ferry for pedestrians. Utter chaos ensued for six weeks while an emergency wooden bridge was erected by the Royal Engineers. In the meantime on the southern side of the Bridge, Craske's office had to be demolished. The harbour cottages were later pulled down to make way for a makeshift road bridge – seen here in the foreground and leading to the extreme right. The photograph is looking towards Commercial Road from the Kirkley side; by this time the old bridge had been removed and cut up for scrap. Its red and white barriers were still in place, however. Of all these emergency crossing links – the footbridge on the Lake Lothing side, even the road bridge in the foreground, which also had quite a sharp bend in it – none remained in place after the new bridge was opened. In fact, Lowestoft was hoping for a four-lane bridge to equal that of Great Yarmouth which had opened forty years before in 1929. The photograph, which was taken in about 1970, also shows a fashion popular at the time – miniskirts. The young mother in her fashionable short shirt and cape, most likely lined with artificial fur, with her little son, just as fashionably dressed, is about to cross to the town centre.

Opposite: The Bascule Bridge, looking north, 1980. Although there were attempts to ease the traffic flow, the peculiarities of this system were, without expanding the width of the road, now three lanes on the bridge – two travelling south into Kirkley, and for some bizarre reason, only one travelling north into the town centre. Traffic queues built up accordingly. *(Ken Carsey)*

The Bascule Bridge was opened in March 1972 by Lowestoft's MP Jim Prior. Although an improvement, with only two lanes the new bridge was somewhat of a disappointment. With heavy vehicles crossing over on both sides it was soon clear that someone had not done their homework. This also meant that there were problems with loads such as this Pickfords Scammell. *(Ken Carsey)*

The main fire station in Normanston Drive, seen here in March 1974, was situated within easy access of the town, its outskirts and to Oulton Broad and to some parts of south Lowestoft, and had come a long way from the old borough fire station in St Peter's Street. The new station was officially opened in 1972 by the Duchess of Kent and was built on the site of Normanhurst, a large mansion used as a fire station during and after the last war. *(Ernest Graystone)*

South Lowestoft fire substation, Beaconsfield Road, 1980. Despite Kirkley's rapid growth, this was South Lowestoft's only fire station up until 2010. On the corner with Clifton Road, the building had been converted as a fire station as part of the National Fire Service war effort. Under the more recent fire station sign to the left of the double doors are two signs dating back to the Second World War. *(Ken Carsey)*

Selling herring at auction from a Scots trawler. Hopes ran high on the Fish Market in 1975 when the Peterhead boat *Faithful II* landed the first herring since the late 1960s. George Thom from Hobson's was the salesman here at this historic auction on the Waveney Dock. Needless to say, despite conservation measures the herring never returned in any great quantity. *(Ernest Graystone)*

North Denes net-drying area, late 1970s. Once, much of the North Denes up to the Corporation Swimming Pool was one large net-drying area. Nets were hung up to dry on these wooden racks, which by the 1970s were being used by fewer and fewer fishermen. The scene here speaks for itself: through lack of use the racks deteriorated even more, slowly disappearing in number as the Birds Eye factory has expanded. The Sea Wall is in the background, *(Ken Carsey)*

Skeldergate under construction at Richards Shipyard, 1976. Built for the Turnbull Scott Shipping Company, this 295ft long chemical tanker could carry approximately 3,500 tonnes and was the largest vessel built at the Lowestoft yard at the time. Because of its size, bad weather delayed the launch for a few days. This did not stop the official launching party, which went ahead on land. Once the weather had improved, she finally slid into the water. Until 1962, Richards had concentrated on building fishing vessels, however, after the decline of the herring stocks in the following years of that decade, the shipyard began building a series of tugs – mainly for J.P. Knight & Co. of Rochester. Although they would build a few more trawlers in future years, Richards customers tended more towards vessels such as tugs, oil rig supply vessels and chemical tankers. Richards was one of six major employers on the South Quay. This would mean that for much of the late 1950s, the 1960s and into the 1970s, Lowestoft had almost all of its population from just under sixteen up to sixty-five years of age in work – the bulk of which was highly skilled. It's fair to say that members of the fairer sex were very particular then, and always looking towards their future security. So much so, that on a Friday night in Arthur's Disco at the Royal Hotel or at the South Pier, when girl met boy the first question asked, 'What's your name?', was not as important as the next: 'And where do you work?' And if there was no job, or the girl didn't think much of your prospects, it was always no girlfriend! *(Ernest Graystone)*

Opposite: Eastern Counties bus station, Gordon Road, 1975. The bus garage was originally the Regent Alfresco Theatre opened in about 1921 and acquired by Eastern Counties in the 1930s. All the buses here have bodies made in Lowestoft by Eastern Coachworks. Located on the northern side of Lake Lothing, the coachworks were founded in 1913. As with all the industries in the town, generation followed generation – son followed father – in working there. *(Ken Carsey)*

Girls at TV Manufacturing, School Road, *c.* 1978. Taken when the Pye factory was part of the Philips group, health and safety did not appear to be much of a concern here! I'm not sure of the event; signs of fish and chips and a few of the girls looking slightly merry and wearing party hats suggest a Christmas party. Mrs Bilverstone is on the left nearest the camera, while the tall girl sitting immediately behind her may be a member of the Fisk family. *(Ken Carsey)*

St Peter's Street looking towards the junction of Clapham Road, 1975. Crisps cycle and motorcycle centre faces Thurston Road opposite. The National Tyre Service moved across to the old Percy Wigg yard (also opposite) not long after this photograph was taken; demolition has already started at the top of Clapham Road. All of the shops seen here would go by August 1977, apart from the terrace in the distance and the buildings on the right. *(Ken Carsey)*

The Anchor of Hope public house, on the eastern side of Clapham Road, *c.* 1975. It was photographed not long before it was demolished to make way for Katwijk Way. The pub was tied to the Yarmouth brewery Lacons. There may have been animosity among fishermen, but when it came to beer it was quite a different story! Regretfully by October 1976 it had become one of Lowestoft's lost pubs. *(Ken Carsey)*

Above: The upper part of Clapham Road, 1976. The silhouette of Rishton House can be seen in the distance. All the premises on the left side of Clapham Road have been demolished and all that's left are the street lamps and the footpath. Opposite, many of the ancient houses remained. The small set-back terrace was built in the early nineteenth century when this part of Clapham Road was known as Shuckford's Loke. *(Ken Carsey)*

Right: The demolition of no. 142 Clapham Road, *c.* 1975. The aptly named Charles Edward Barber had been a gentlemen's hairdresser at no. 142 since at least 1948. Edward Booty had the shop from 1935 until the war. Only four doors up from Ada Roe's Dairy at 136 Clapham Road, this shop, as well as Ada Roe's, were all demolished by late 1976 to make way for the new spinal road.
(Ken Carsey)

The Silver Jubilee of Queen Elizabeth II, 1977: the bunting is out and so are the royal portraits. This branch of Walker-Regis, which had been a Barclay's Bank until 1964, was on the corner of London Road North and Commercial Road. A dealer in fancy goods and leather travel goods, as well as holiday souvenirs, it was in an ideal position for the passing holiday trade. In the doorway is a display of postcards, buckets and spades, sandals and beach balls. And not forgetting the famous Lowestoft rock (I was never too sure if it was made by Foreman's of Pakefield or Docwra's in Great Yarmouth). The windows were always crammed full with jewellery, ceramics and brass work. I once bought a cheap brass straight trumpet or post-horn in there which (surprisingly) worked – after a fashion! Next door in Commercial Road is one of the budding holiday and travel shops then springing up – a sign that the town's economy was quite buoyant. A fashion note on the young man passing the Mini and walking towards Walker-Regis' doorway; flares and platform shoes were the in thing at the time, as was the hairstyle. By the time of the Silver Jubilee, New Elizabethans of both sexes had become members of the Flower Power generation. Even old and crinkly thirty-year-olds like yours truly would be seen with suits of a similar cut as this young man's, flares (naturally) and long hair – although the young man here had a better hair fashion that I did, and those shoes! I can confirm they did cripple you, especially when you slid off them – as I was apt to do! *(Ken Carsey)*

Above: Stern trawler LT144 *St Phillip* about to leave for the North Sea fishing grounds, 1976. A chance to compare the old with the new, both vessels were owned by the Colne Fishing Company. Moored in the Trawl Dock itself is one of Colne's older side trawlers with its name and fishing registration painted out, about to join Gordon Claridge's fleet of gas rig standby vessels. *(Author)*

Right: The old Waveney Herring and Mackerel Dock, 1976. This photograph was taken one Saturday afternoon, when boats had yet to arrive for unloading for Monday morning's auction. There had been discussions of a new enlarged market for many years. Development had started in the late 1960s on the Trawl Dock. While there were improvements on the Waveney Dock in the late 1970s, the new enclosed Waveney Market which opened in 1987 came too late. *(Author)*

Dove Street from St Margaret's Plain, 1978, with the High Street in the far distance. The houses on the right are all that is left of medieval and early Tudor Lowestoft apart from buildings in the High Street itself and St Margaret's Church. The First and Last public house is on the extreme right. Since this photograph was taken at least two of the smaller premises shown on the right have been demolished. *(Author)*

No. 196 Yarmouth Road, Gunton, March 1979. I must admit I know very little of 1930s post-modernist house building in Lowestoft apart from what survived after the war, the best remembered being the 'Dutchman's House' in Corton Road, begun in 1939 and demolished well before I could hold a camera. This house may also have been built in the 1930s, or was influenced by pre-war designs – I never did find out. *(Author)*

3
THE 1980s
THE BEGINNING OF THE END

Richards Ironworks had celebrated its centenary in 1976 and was looking forward to another hundred years of successful shipbuilding. In the early 1980s, Richards and their colleagues in Heath Road – Brooke Marine – continued the age-old tradition of sons following fathers into a highly skilled trade. Cyril Potter looks at the camera – but what is noticeable is the confidence of the young men nearby. *(Ken Carsey)*

Peter Catchpole (left) and an unnamed Rossfish Grimsby senior representative, c. 1980. In fact Mr Catchpole does not look too confident and had good reason to be cautious as the following years would prove. High-intensity trawling would do as much damage as herring overfishing did in the early 1960s.
(Ernest Graystone)

Harold Critten, Engineering Department, Richards Shipyard, August 1981. Old hands such as Mr Critten passed on their skills and expertise honed over the decades to a new generation of apprentices. Everything was made by hand on site – every ship was different and needed experienced and expert craftsmen to build them.
(Ken Carsey)

CWS No. 2 factory and Lowestoft Canning, November 1981. Seen here from the top of one of Richards' cranes, these were just two of the factories along the South Quay alone which employed an estimated 15,000 men and women. Almost all were located next to each other: Morton's, Jewson, Richards Ironworks, CWS (including Lowestoft Canning), Boulton & Paul, Brooke Marine and Pye. The big chimney belonged to the CWS No. 2 factory. *(Ken Carsey)*

Looking south across Kirkley Fen, the view from one of Richards' cranes, November 1981. The view is across the dam built in 1894 by the Maconochie brothers linking Horn Hill with Waveney Drive, with Kirkley Ham stretching off into the distance. Durban Road is upper right. The Ham was and still is an active river. At the rear of the garage the terrain remains marshy. *(Ken Carsey)*

Suffolk Road, October 1980. A poignant scene showing some smaller businesses reliant on the Fish Market; Conroy's newsagents is on the extreme left; K.G. Ellis where fishermen and visitors alike bought their footwear; General Accident insurance office; the Singer sewing machine shop; and finally Lynn House, a small property for decades home to Bird's cycle shop. Later it became part of Tuttle's department store. *(Ken Carsey)*

Bevan Street East, 1980. Waveney Insurance Brokers is the shop on the left; the rather dilapidated upper storeys of the shop in the centre belong to H.W. Sparham, newsagents and purveyor of cards and souvenirs. In the 1920s this was a branch of Fredrick Norton's. On the right is Coes 'mans shop', which as Ernest Long's fisherman's outfitters in the late 1950s and early '60s also made Lowestoft's unique fishermen's suits. *(Ken Carsey)*

London Road South, looking south from Grosvenor Road, 1981. The fact that it was November explains the lack of traffic coming towards the camera. Even then, there were still people about. The long roof-line belongs to the Grand Bingo Hall. The Fina petrol station has now been replaced by a KFC drive-in. The petrol prices are interesting to note: £1.64 for two-star and £1.66.9 for four-star. And these prices are for gallons, not litres! *(Ken Carsey)*

Looking across to the silo on the North Quay, 1981. Seen from the top of the same crane used on page 47, and looking north towards St Margaret's Church; the light coloured terraces behind the silo are in Denmark Road. The silo is still there today, thus giving a good idea as to where this particular crane once stood. As the photograph was taken in November, it must have been bitterly cold up there. *(Ken Carsey)*

Waveney Fish Market, *c.* 1980. To the outsider, boats were landing as usual; however, the numbers of landings were declining not just because of the increasing cost of fuel but declining fish stocks. Plaice and haddock remained plentiful and by the mid-1970s the first 'beamer' trawlers were fishing out of the port. *Pescoco II* is seen here about to moor up. Other vessels in the background include LT251 *St Croix* which was eventually scrapped in 1986. *(Ernest Graystone)*

The Yacht Basin, June 1980. Not only is the Lowestoft lifeboat *Fredrick Edward Crick* moored in the Yacht Basin, but so is a pilot boat to its right. The port was rapidly changing over to North Sea gas and oil rigs standby duties, hence the lack of fishing registrations on the boats in the Trawl Dock. Nearest the camera are two inflatable rescue boats – one belonging to the Colne Group and the one behind it to Putford. *(Author)*

Lowestoft Trawl Dock, 1980. Ann Hubbard, a packer from the nearby Rossfish factory, takes a break along the quayside. The dock was packed with trawlers from Boston Deep Sea, Small & Co., Colne, and a multitude of smaller companies. Some were on standby duties but many were still fishing. In the background, centre left, is the Bridge terrace, while on the right is Commercial Road. Because the photograph was taken with a telephoto lens, the silo in Commercial Road looks larger than it actually is. Ross employed an average of 180 men and women, if not more, full-time and part-time, and its processing plant was the largest on the Fish Market. Initially, as far as I recall, the reason why Ross closed was largely a matter of trimming non-profitable branches. It was a battle between Lowestoft and Hull – we lost and within a year of this photograph, the Ross office, which was behind the photographer, had closed. The processing factory followed in March 1982. *(Author)*

Waveney Dock, 1980. Beam trawler LT266 *Semper Crescendo* appears to be the only one fishing in this photograph. As if ignoring each other, at least two of the other boats, *Oulton Queen* and *Farnham Queen* appear to be preparing for standby duties. The tug is the *Finch*, registered in London. The flotsam and jetsam in the water around the beam trawler are a reminder (if any were needed) that the dock was not a pleasant place to fall into! *(Author)*

Widening the channel into the Inner Harbour, 1980. Both Richards and Brooke Marine were building ever-larger ships. Cargo vessels using the port were also increasing in size. At one time Lowestoft had its own full-time dredger, *Lake Lothing*, but now the channel itself had to be widened. The photographer does not say whether the work was just on the northern side, seen here with warehouses and buildings in Commercial Road in the background. *(Ken Carsey)*

AK Diesels Ltd, Shelton Works, Salisbury Road, 1980. AKD was founded by Alick King who had started his working life at Richards in 1924. After marrying one of Sam Richards' daughters, he set up his own business in 1932 in conjunction with W.H. Podd building diesel engines to his own design. Seen here is the main workshop in Salisbury Road. Parked next to the fence is a Honda light van. *(Ken Carsey)*

AKD Engineering, *c.* 1980. This is one of a series of photographs taken in the AKD workshop by photographer Ernest Graystone. These two anonymous engineers are working on a piece of machinery in the Salisbury Road workshop. Everything was built by hand by skilled craftsmen. AKD maintained a connection with Richards when in 1949 Alick King designed and built a new type of diesel engine for LT310 *WFP*.

Fruit and vegetable merchants, Love Road, 1981. Situated between Beresford Road and Raglan Street, this shop was not far from the Crown Meadow football ground. W.R. Meades had the shop as a grocer's in 1969. To the left is the grandly named Flixton Lodge. *(Ken Carsey)*

The off-licence on the corner of Stanley Street, 1981. Off-licences were once the feature of many street corners, especially in the Stanley Street and Norwich Road area. Changes in shopping habits, coupled with the closure of Eastern Coachworks not far away in 1986, meant that many small corner shops including off-licences, were to close. This one, I'm pleased to say, although slightly changed, still survives today. *(Ken Carsey)*

Right: **The Call of the Sea** bronze sculpture by William Redgrave. This figure of a fisherman had borne the brunt of many jokes since its erection in the 1970s in front of Tuttles department store in London Road North. By the time this photograph was taken in March 1981, an assortment of objects had been hung from his left arm including plastic bags, bras, bottles and telephone directories! Tuttles itself was about to close after nearly a hundred years. *(Ken Carsey)*

Below: Following the opening of the Asda supermarket on the South Quay in about 2008 on what fifteen years before had been Richards Shipyard, the statue was moved to the nearby Promenade. Although still pointing the wrong way – the late Jack Rose once told me he was supposed to be pointing out to sea – he has a new plinth and only the seagulls to contend with. Across Lake Lothing is the silo on the North Quay. *(Author)*

London Road North, July 1981. The best-remembered event of the year was the wedding of Prince Charles and Lady Diana Spencer. Not very clear from this vantage point, but Tesco's had decked their windows in all its royal wedding finery. In 1981, buses still travelled up the street to drop off at the 'Arcade' outside the Journal office. *(Ken Carsey)*

Royal wedding decorations at the cycle and moped shop on the corner of Beaconsfield Road. Shops and houses were all bedecked in July 1981, proving that you didn't have to be a big company to show your appreciation and best wishes to the royal couple. Every red-blooded New Elizabethan male was extremely envious of Prince Charles. *(Ken Carsey)*

Above: W.H. Smith's new store dedicated part of its side window facing the Prairie to the royal couple, promoting the latest available in souvenirs. In London Road North, the pedestrian precinct was yet to be built and buses were still able to travel up and down the town centre. *(Ken Carsey)*

Right: Although the royal wedding took place in July 1981, celebrations continued during that year's carnival a few weeks later in August. In those days, carnival processions travelled from Pakefield in the south, up London Road South, passing Grosvenor Road where the photographer stood, across the Bridge to north Lowestoft, along Katwijk Way and Jubilee Way ending at one time at North Parade. As the years went by, the route got shorter. *(Ken Carsey)*

McCarthy's, Lorne Park Road, 1981. Businesses large and small were to be found around the town supplying the resort and the town's fishing industry. McCarthy's, with its local warehouse on the corner of Richmond Road and Lorne Park Road, was one of several Norwich businesses with branches in Lowestoft. Note the VW estate parked behind the petrol pump. *(Ken Carsey)*

Ronnie Cook's family butchers, 41 and 42 High Street, c. 1981. The freezer centre was added in the 1970s. Both Cook's and Baxters next door (to the right) were two of the longer-established businesses in this part of the town. Bayfield's were butchers at no. 41 in 1927, but Ronnie Cook took over in 1938. The shop is seen here not long before its refurbishment. Baxter's, at nos 43 and 44, dated back even further to the 1860s. A.W. Smith had the premises as a butchers and grocers at least up to 1959. Johnny Belton then took over the shop from 1963. Ronnie Cook's premises stood on the corner of Mariners Score. As the Swanne Inn it was famous for having Oliver Cromwell stay there in March 1643 during the short and fortunately bloodless siege of the town. Little is left of the inn save for the medieval cellars; however, like most of Lowestoft's High Street buildings, especially on the cliff side, it has a considerable amount of early remains from older buildings in its structure. Ronnie Cook's closed in 1985. Regretfully it has now lost the doorway in the centre of the premises and the legend Cromwell House. Mariners Score, the alleyway to the left of Ronnie Cook's, was once part of an ancient track that led from the Denes along Church Road past St Margaret's Church and into Oulton. The reflection in the freezer centre's window is the Blue Anchor on the corner of Mariners Street. *(Ken Carsey)*

Opposite: Looking east across Lowestoft from Richards, November 1981. The view overlooks the terraces of St John's Road, Marine Parade and the houses on the Esplanade. Mill Road is in the centre of the photograph. Looking down, we also see Richards Shipyard in Horn Hill, complete with sheets of metal waiting to be cut up, warehouses and workshops. M.R. King's garage and petrol station next to Richards face the National filling station opposite. *(Ken Carsey)*

Rossfish factory and office, Trawl Market, early 1982. By this time the Ross logo has been removed from the office front. It came as a shock to the people of Lowestoft when the Ross factory finally closed in March 1982 with the loss of 150 jobs. The administration block had already gone the previous November, although parts were still in use as late as 1986 when one of the smaller fish companies had their walk-in freezer unit there! *(Author)*

The royal wedding clock, London Road North, c. 1983. The area later became part of Queen Elizabeth Place. The clock was erected as part of the town centre's new pedestrian precinct and quickly became popular as a place to meet. Both visitors and locals had a high regard for this black monolith of a clock tower which commemorated the wedding of Prince Charles and Lady Diana Spencer in 1981. In September 1997 it became the centre of the town's mourning following the death of the princess; there must have been hundreds of wreaths and bunches of flowers laid at the foot of the clock in the days leading up to her funeral and beyond. *(Ken Carsey)*

Opposite: Whatever was happening on the Fish Market, shipbuilding at Richards Ironworks in Horn Hill looked set to continue unabated. Looking towards the CWS Waveney Fine Foods canning factory in Riverside Road, the launching and the subsequent fitting out of the *Seagair* in 1982 allowed shipwrights, staff and guests to admire the new vessel. *(Ken Carsey)*

Waiting for the Bridge, 1983. Pier Terrace is on the left, the Bascule Bridge is in the middle and the Harbour Hotel, still with its early Victorian entrance and then known as the Bridge House, is on the right behind Notleys Royal Thoroughfare Auction Showrooms. A precarious junction even now, four lanes of traffic (two north and two south) had to cross a three-lane road bridge. *(Ken Carsey)*

A closer look at the Bascule Bridge at the time shows the problem more clearly. Not the straying pedestrian, I hasten to add. Although there appears to be enough room for an extra lane on the landward side, those travelling from Kirkley towards the town centre could only use one northbound lane. The Bridge terrace, part of Station Square, is on the left. Commercial Road is centre left, while the bridge control house and Waveney Road are on the right. *(Ken Carsey)*

Looking northwards to the Bascule Bridge from Royal Plain, *c.* 1984. Two lanes from the north travel past the Royal Plain and the Bridge House and head south along Marine Parade. I defy anyone to explain this one lane north and two lanes south arrangement! *(Ken Carsey)*

Built in Renfrew in 1972 and eventually sold to Putford as a standby vessel, LT94 *Boston Sea Dart* is seen here entering the Trawl Basin, mid-1970s. Lowestoft's fishing fleet was rapidly changing; even the safer stern trawlers were being retired or turned over to standby duties. Once, the inconvenience of the Bridge was a spectacle watched by visitors and residents alike, standing at the rails observing the fishing boats passing through on their way out to sea, but all this would all change. *(Ernest Graystone)*

Jarrolds Office Equipment Centre, corner of Beach Road and Grove Road, 1984. Beach Road is on the right. Built in the mid-1890s for J. Flood, printer and bookbinders, it became part of Jarrolds in the 1970s. The main shop was located in London Road North, only yards away. On offer in the Grove Road window nearest the door is a range of new drawing boards. *(Ken Carsey)*

Tonning Street, 1983. Looking at the southern side of the thoroughfare, the shop nearest to the camera was called the Bear's Parlour, a previous occupant sold toy bears as well as antiques. Although businesses suffered when the street was cut off from the town centre by Katwijk Way in 1976, this shop became my philatelic, postcard and printed ephemera emporium from 1982 to May 1984. *(Author)*

Looking south from outside St Margaret's churchyard, the highest point in Lowestoft, 1984. Spruce Court was under construction when I took this photograph. To the centre right is the chimney of the Co-op factory in Riverside Road as well as the two water towers in Pakefield. Things only changed in 2010 with the building of Lowestoft's first sixth form college in Rotterdam Road. *(Author)*

North Denes Market and fun fare, April 1985. April traditionally used to be the month when the funfair reached Lowestoft. For one week, the Denes were a blaze of noise and colour. In 1985 the fair was also accompanied also by a general market with clothes, bric-a-brac, sweets and burger stands. It was supposed to be a day out on a Lowestoft College assignment, but who could resist it? *(Author)*

Business premises in St Peter's Street, *c.* 1980. Located opposite Water Lane, this pair of shops always intrigued me and obviously the photographer, wondering whether or not there was any connection between the two! A.W. Critoph was a butcher here in 1947, followed by W.M. Foster by 1951. Jack Pritchard was here by 1958 and continued through the 1960s. Powell's had been an undertaker here since before 1927. *(Ken Carsey)*

The queen's visit in June 1985 was basically to perform two official duties; firstly to open the town's new museum at Nicholas Everett Park, and secondly to officially name the area around the royal wedding clock Queen Elizabeth Place. Prince Philip stands not far away admiring the flower bed. In the background people, press and shop assistants take advantage of any roof space they can get. *(Author)*

Skipper Victor Vigo di Gallidoro, July 1985. Seen here in front of Waveney Dock, di Gallidoro built up a fleet of beam trawlers, among them the *De Vrouw Melanie*. In 1992 he became a victim of what many in the fishing industry considered a case for concern when his bank called in a loan and receivers sold *De Vrouw Melanie*, one of three trawlers worth an estimated £1.5 million, to the Dutch for £360. *(Ernest Graystone)*

The final days of Brooke Marine as seen from Leathes Ham on the opposite side of Lake Lothing, January 1987. Although several ships are moored close by, the cranes stand idle in an area which only ten years before had been expanded to meet a new era. Renamed Brooke Yachts International and despite building such high-profile boats as Richard Branson's *Virgin Atlantic Challenger II*, the yard finally closed in 1993. *(Author)*

The view looking across to south Lowestoft and Carlton Colville and the Broads, *c.* 1986. The cranes of Richards shipyard and Brooke Marine break the skyline. The windowless block on the right in the foreground then housed Lowestoft College's oil and gas rig training pool. Out of the photograph on the left was the new Maritime block designed to resemble a ship. Between the new block and Newson's Meadow is the students' car park. The panorama also shows not only Lowestoft Cemetery – the upper quarter of the photograph, with the cemetery lodge – but also Minden Road, Rotterdam Road and Eastern Coachworks, the latter then in its final months. On the horizon are Carlton Colville and the nearby Norfolk Broads. Newson's Meadow became the last of the borough's council houses to be built before the war. The cemetery is the final resting place of several of the town's notables, in particular the Maconochie brothers, and also many of the victims of the 1942 Waller Raid. *(Author)*

Lowestoft Art Centre, seen here in August 1979, was Lowestoft College's School of Art annex. Located on the corner of Regent Road and Alexandra Road, it housed life study studios, a screen printing workshop, lecture rooms, gallery and a multitude of classrooms. Catering for the serious artist and for those who had hopes for an artistic career, John Raey, Jo Budd, Mick Sparksman and illustrator Simon Colby studied or taught here. *(Ken Carsey)*

Lowestoft Art Centre gallery, 1987. Each year the centre displayed students' final or degree work. Invitations would go to guests from all parts of the art world as far afield as Falmouth, an area greatly favoured by Lowestoft students. This anonymous student is admiring the work of a number of now-famed potters who exhibited that year – among whom were the Greengrass twins, Graham Bloice and Ann Hubbard. *(Author)*

Eastern Coachworks, Eastern Way, January 1987. Considered to be one of the giants of British bus builders, Eastern Coachworks' closure in late 1986 stunned the town. Problems had grown over the previous few years, added to which deregulation had led to the break-up of the National Bus Company, ECW's main customer. Operators now bought elsewhere and the decline for specially built bus bodies set in. Bulldozers moved in to demolish the factory in February 1989. *(Author)*

Three new Eastern National buses pose outside Eastern Coachworks in much happier days in 1979. Originally founded in 1913 as United, it became famous for its quality of design and its workmanship. As with Richards Ironworks and Brooke Marine, son followed father into employment here, in a continuous line down the generations. *(Ernest Graystone)*

A Leyland National ECW stops outside the old police station and police courts in Regent Road, October 1989. One of the coachworks' best-known designs could still be found in Lowestoft and in other parts of the country into the 1990s. The police court moved to Old Nelson Street in May 1989 and the bus stop later became a taxi rank. *(Author)*

This half-cab ECW-built Bristol, seen at the old Gordon Road bus station, was somewhat of a rare sight even in 1985. Its fleet number was FLF 466, but what its fate was I am unable to ascertain. However, over the years, several of these earlier ECWs found their way abroad as open-top tourist attractions as far afield as New Zealand, the United States and Canada (where they are described as London buses!), as well as the Russian Federation! *(Author)*

The Prairie, the site of today's Britten Centre, not long before demolition started in 1986. Located off London Road North, opposite the Marina, Howards estate agents was at nos 1 and 2, while Hanby Williams – also an estate agent – to the right, was in a post-war building replacing the old coach house of 91 London Road North. W.H. Smith is on the extreme right where the Ford Escort is parked. *(Ken Carsey)*

Looking the length of the Prairie towards Martins in London Road North. A temporary car park is situated between W.H. Smith's and the Premier Laundry, the building on the right close to the camera. The Premier became the town's first museum which was subsequently transferred to Nicholas Everett Park in 1985. If my memory serves me correctly, the building with the double doors on the left temporarily housed a photographic exhibition by historian Jack Rose. *(Ken Carsey)*

Waiting for the carnival procession, August 1989. For the greater part of its existence, Lowestoft's carnival procession used to travel from Pakefield, through the town and up to North Parade. The opening of Katwijk Way in 1977 meant that the procession no long travelled through the town centre but came up the new road, turning off at Milton Road East, opposite to Milton Road West which can be seen here on the left. *(Author)*

Steam rollers, Alexandra Road, August, 1989. That year a shortened carnival procession was made up (at least for fans of traction engines) by two entries from the East Anglian Transport Museum taking on water outside the Adrian Works. The Aveling & Porter (RT2474) once belonged to Lowestoft Borough Corporation; behind it is an Armstrong Whitworth towing a workman's caravan. Photographers had a whale of a time that afternoon! *(Author)*

Mutford Lock Bridge as seen from the Oulton side. This and the following three views were taken in 1989. This is Lowestoft's only other road bridge across Lake Lothing and was opened in 1939 just as war broke out. Looking over the road from Hallidays the Chemist, Bridge Road Greengrocery is on the left facing Commodore Road. By the late 1980s, it was clear that with the huge numbers of vehicles using the bridge, it was rapidly approaching the end of its life.

The shops in Bridge Road seen from Commodore Road. Hallidays is on the corner on the extreme left. The American Style Restaurant was still in business, as was Bridge Road Greengrocery, Burger House restaurant appears also still in business. At the entrance to the back of the shops is a sign announcing 'Gay Dogs' which was a dog grooming parlour. All these shops were swept away to make way for the new bridge and bypass.

Bridge Road from Victoria Road junction. The Carlton Colville side of Mutford Lock Bridge had the added problem of congestion at these traffic lights. Oulton Broad is the only route from Lowestoft to Norwich. Holiday traffic, factories and shipyards in Horn Hill, Waveney Drive and Victoria Road itself, not forgetting the railway crossing, meant queues were common. The houses facing the camera survived but the cottages on the right went to make way for the bypass and bridge.

Bridge Road, Oulton Broad. Looking towards Victoria Road junction, it was very quiet here in the early weeks of spring but extremely busy later on during the resort's summer season. The Dutch-style church and the scout hut next door were all swept away, as was Taylors the newsagents on the corner; however the fish and chip restaurant is still with us.

Lowestoft Bascule Bridge, seen from the southern side, October 1989. Pier Terrace is on the left with Williams Restaurant at the junction of Belvedere Road, also on the left. Notleys Auction Rooms had closed and the premises were used for a number of projects including language taster classes. Here we see a typical traditional Lowestoft 'Bridger', a word synonymous with the town's road headache; as far as I know the word is unique to the Lowestoft area. Once a good excuse to be late for work or for that important appointment that you really didn't want to go to, 'Bridgers' in the days of the old Swing Bridge were more acceptable. We expected its replacement to be more like that at Great Yarmouth (which is a four-lane road bridge), but the extraordinary lack of knowledge by the planners who completely ignored what Lowestoft needed, meant that by 1989 the phrase 'Bridger' meant – at least to those crossing from Kirkley – endless queues waiting to get to the town centre. It is clear in this photograph what the problem has always been – three lanes to serve a four-lane road system. The consultation the following year (1990) for a third crossing confirmed the Riverside Road and Denmark Road option, but there the problem was the town's railway station. The Bascule Bridge remains the only road bridge in the town itself crossing Lake Lothing; the proposed second crossing linking Riverside Road and Denmark Road never happened, nor it seems will it ever, regretfully for the people of Lowestoft and for businesses who wish to settle here. *(Author)*

4

THE 1990s
THE END OF AN ERA

Sparrow's Nest Gardens bowling green in August 1990 was as popular as ever. Older players may be on the green, but would-be younger future participants look on. Beyond the old cottage which houses Lowestoft's famous Maritime Museum, and looking towards the Sea Wall, can be seen the Denes Caravan Camp, always full with holidaymakers, many enjoying the brisk walk up the Scores into the High Street.
(Author)

Sparrow's Nest Theatre in its last summer, August 1990. Its final theatrical season was in 1988 when singer and guitarist Joe Brown topped the bill. Despite its historic importance, not only did singers and actors of the calibre of Paul Robeson and Leslie Hutchinson appear here, it also played an important part during the Second World War as the Royal Naval Patrol Service land station HMS *Europa*. Despite protests, the theatre was demolished in 1991. *(Author)*

Lowestoft Revival Smack Race and fête, Royal Green, June 1996. The Lydia Eva Trust was then in its infancy, but those who wished to help to fund the project had the honour of talking to Lydia Eva herself! Then in her eighties, Lydia Eva Cocks (the elderly lady on the left) was only a young girl when she launched the steam drifter *Lydia Eva* for her father, Harry Eastick, in Kings Lynn in 1930. *(Author)*

Belle Vue Park lodge was virtually destroyed in February 1990 when vandals set the thatched roof alight. The occupant, Mr Alec Haig, the park's gardener, managed to get out just in time. Built when the park was laid out in 1874, the town was determined that the lodge would be rebuilt as near to the original as possible. *(Author)*

Royal Green fête with the Royal Norfolk and Suffolk Yacht Club in the background, *c.* 1990. In the early 1990s there had been several suggestions over what should happen to the Royal Green. Since the demolition of the Royal Hotel in 1973, the area between the Yacht Club and Tides Reach on the Esplanade was little more than a broad empty space. Ideas included a bowling alley and a sports centre, but to no avail. Eventually it was decided on a new pavilion. Here, however, that decision was some time away. *(Author)*

Eastern Counties Ford Minibus, 1990. A new breed of bus enabled a better service in the town as well as the ability to cover routes where larger buses were unable to go. Seen here at the town centre terminus outside the Tesco supermarket is the 103 on the Oulton village via Church Road circuit. Although popular, their major drawback was that they could only hold nineteen passengers. *(Author)*

Eastern Counties Ford Minibus in Harris Avenue, 1990. The bus is picking up a passenger on the 100 route, a route that included the High Street as well as the town centre. This was one of the busier routes of the service. Again, the size of the bus meant only a limited number of passengers could be carried at any one time. *(Author)*

The older style of Eastern Counties ECW-bodied bus in the Britten Centre bus station, July 1990. Many of these older style Bristols were broken up, but some, possibly this one, joined their half-cab sisters as tourist attractions around the world, or extended their working lives as works buses in England. *(Author)*

Open-top Leyland VR in Harris Avenue, 1992. Several of these Leyland VR/ECWs were converted to summer use. OCK 995K was of 1973 vintage and despite the dull weather – it rained that day – the novelty of an open deck meant that some did not mind a minor drenching! Route 100 kept north of the Bascule Bridge which enabled it to run as a 5–10-minute service. *(Author)*

Adrian Works, Alexandra Road, May 1990. This is where Brooke Marine all began. Founded in 1874, J.W. Brooke remained on this site until the 1930s. East Anglian Engineering had the factory after the war, but by 1963 Swallow Prams were here. Following closure in the 1970s, several small businesses used parts of the site until it was decided in 1990 to demolish the old buildings. Only this block survived, seen here as part of the Youth Training Service. *(Author)*

Adrian Works, Alexandra Road, May 1990. Demolition started on this block at the end of April 1990, following unsuccessful attempts to keep the building functioning as a sports centre. Alexandra Road Surgery now stands on the site where motoring pioneer Maudsley Brooke, the son of J.W. Brooke, produced the first Brooke car and where the famous Brooke Swan car was built. *(Author)*

The upper part of the High Street, *c.* 1991. The opening of Jubilee Way in 1977 gradually turned this part of the High Street into a residential area, although a veterinary surgery, a dental surgery, one photographer and some small restaurants survived. One shop in the block on the right, identified by the grand double first- and second-floor bay windows, had already been turned into flats. Today most of this side of the High Street is residential. *(Author)*

The war memorial, Royal Plain, looking towards the Bascule Bridge, September 1990. Lowestoft's war memorial was erected in 1921 in memory of those who fell in the First World War. It had added poignancy following the Second World War and continues as a memorial to all of those who have died in action since. The art deco bus shelter, moved here in June 1939, is now in the East Anglian Transport Museum. *(The late Joan Agnes Plant)*

Wherry Hotel, Oulton Broad, 1991. Construction of the new bridge and bypass (on the right) has already started at the time of this photograph. Looking across to the Oulton side of the only Norfolk Broad in Suffolk, the Wherry Hotel opened in 1897, then as now, the centre for the start of any Broads holiday. Moored along the Free Quay on the other side of the modern cruiser on the left is the houseboat *Doris*, built in 1931 by J.W. Brooke. *(Author)*

North Lowestoft from St Peter's Court, early 1990s. The first thing one is aware of here is that there are no wind turbines on the horizon off Yarmouth (on the left). Taken from the roof of the sixteen-storey high-rise building before the roof became encumbered with aerials big enough to turn the area into a glorified microwave oven, the road in the centre of the photograph is Park Road which leads to Yarmouth Road and the Belle Vue Park. The car park in the foreground is in Church Road and the terrace of six council houses on the right was built in the 1960s. Until the late 1950s Mariners Street (on the right out of the photograph) led directly into Church Road. On the right are the flats bordering Park Road, Melbourne Road and the Hemplands. The four blocks in the bottom right and the row of what look like outhouses are in fact sheds, and were built on the site of several medieval and Tudor houses including buildings connected to the Lowestoft witch trials of 1662. St Peter's Court itself was constructed on part of the site of the Lowestoft China Factory's barn. Breaking the horizon along Yarmouth Road can be seen from right to left; the High Light, the modern spire of Trinity Methodist Church and, in Belle Vue Park, the Royal Naval Patrol Service memorial. *(Author)*

Opposite: Looking across to the Oulton side of the Bridge, 1991. Young holidaymakers walk across the Bridge towards Oulton Broad. Lake Lothing is to the right where the cranes are building the new bridge and bypass. The modern tall building on the left in the background in Bridge Road belonged to Hoseasons. All the buildings on the right were demolished to make way for the new bridge. *(Author)*

Lowestoft Central station, c. 1990. Lowestoft railway station had its roof removed in 1992 after years of neglect by British Rail. Once it was a vibrant station, a terminus full of life; holidaymakers, commuters, workers travelling to and from Norwich, the Midlands, London and Ipswich – they all made their way through this station. Regretfully, by 1991 there were only two regular services – to Norwich and Ipswich. *(Author)*

Lowestoft station, July 1995. The Ipswich train is on the left and the half-hourly Norwich train on the right. Upgrading the station also meant the loss of its roof. No longer was there a direct link with the capital and the Ipswich train now ran on a single line. In the 1950s there were queues waiting for the train; on this day in July 1995, there were around fifteen people, all waiting to board the Norwich sprinter. *(Author)*

Weston Road and Crestview Surgery seen from the corner of Somerleyton Road and Oulton Road, 1992. Believed to be the remnants of an ancient track linking Flixton St Michael with Gunton St Peter, as the housing estate in the distance expanded nearer to Oulton Road, the track was either removed or realigned. The land on the left of Ann Hubbard is now part of the Aldi supermarket car park in Millennium Way. *(Author)*

Winsor & Newton Crown Brush Works, Crown Street West, 1993. Originally built as Morse & Woods brewery on the site of the old Lowestoft China Factory, this is one important industry that, at the time of writing, I'm pleased to say is still with us and has been here since 1949. The Victorian single-storey block was later demolished to make way for a staff car park. Crown Street Hall is the light coloured building on the same side next to the factory. *(Author)*

Corner shop, Ipswich Road, July 1993. Located on the corner of Ipswich Road and St Margaret's Road; until the middle of the 1990s almost every community had its corner shop. Some, like St Margaret's Road, had several. In the late 1950s you could find a post office, greengrocery, newsagent, tobacconist and sweet shop, public house (two if you count the Belle Vue public house on the corner of St Margaret's Road and the High Street), barber, schools and, at the western end, St Margaret's parish church. Close at hand were chippies, fish yards, yet more public houses, a pet store (Sussex Road), newsagents, butchers and a whole host of general stores and bakeries. Over the years many disappeared; eating habits changed and at least one Chinese takeaway has replaced many of the old chippies although two still survive today. A Mr Wood had this particular shop in 1958 as a grocer; later, in 1969 Hotchkinson's retained it as a greengrocery, and although it still sold fruit and vegetables in the 1990s, as the Jug and Bottle it also ventured into other things. Closing in 2011, the shop was converted into flats. *(Author)*

Opposite: The new bridge's subway under flood, Oulton Broad, February 1993. Looking underneath the new bridge and bypass towards the lock gates, what normally would have been the footpath is on the right, while Lake Lothing itself is between the rails and the bridge. It was evident that the subway was built too close to the tide line. Here it almost disappeared under the Broads tidal surge that morning. *(Author)*

The Yacht Station and Broadway, Oulton Broad, under flood, 1993. Looking across from the comparative high ground of Bridge Road towards the Yacht Station with the trees of Nicholas Everett Park, the only clue as to where the Broad started and the footpath ended is the bow on the extreme right belonging to the houseboat *Doris* which at that date had seen much better days. *(Author)*

The Roger Harrod carpet shop, High Street, 1993. The tall building was known to an earlier generation as the London Drapery Stores. This closed in 1962, becoming Tailorite House Furnishings by 1967. Harrods transferred to the North Denes Industrial Estate in 1998; it then became O'Reilly's public house, famous for its long bar. Looking from St Peter's Street, a lone car is passing Record Revival which was then up for let. *(Author)*

The demolition of shops at the junction of London Road North and High Street, May 1993. Seen from the top of Old Nelson Street, Birds Eye's articulated lorries were having problems travelling down the Ravine to reach the factory on the Denes. As an important part of the town's economy and to ensure the company would not have to move elsewhere, a new route to Whapload Road had to be built enabling larger vehicles easier access to the factory. *(Author)*

Barber Richmore bought the old CWS factory on the corner of Riverside Road in 1994. The company already had a reputation as an asset-stripper when after five months of taking over, in October 1994, they closed the Lowestoft Canning Factory (to the right). The block seen here in May 1995 was finally closed in 1997. Demolition began less than twelve months later. (Author)

East Point Pavilion, Esplanade. Not all was doom and gloom in the 1990s. Seen here in May 2000, the new Pavilion was built on the site of the Royal Hotel which had been demolished in 1973. Costing over £1 million and despite the occasional planning glitch – the original draft plans had indicated a far grander construction – it was eventually opened with great ceremony in May 1993 by the actress Susan Tully. (Author)

Lowestoft Canning Factory, seen here from Waveney Drive in May 1995, had been taken over with the Co-op's other factory (seen on the extreme left) by Barber Richmore in May 1994. Part of Chivers Hartley, they lived up to their reputation for asset-stripping and closing down once-flourishing factories. In October 1994, five months later, they closed down Lowestoft Canning and gave the workforce fifteen minutes to clear the premises. Coming hard on the tail of the closure of the neighbouring Richards Shipyard in May 1994, and the loss of Brooke Marine, Morton's and Eastern Coachworks, for the first time since the 1930s communities all over Lowestoft began to suffer deprivation and social unrest. *(Author)*

Richards Shipyard, Horn Hill, viewed here from the forecourt of the Dial-a-Ride headquarters. The demolition of Lowestoft Canning in 1998 left a unobstructed view of the now empty sheds and silent cranes of Richards. Also gone in one fell swoop of official vandalism and with no thought of its historic importance was the plaque erected in 1894 by the Maconochie brothers to commemorate the linking of west Lowestoft to south Lowestoft with the erection of the road across Kirkley Ham, a river which still is active to this day. Looking across Lake Lothing at this point, the silo in Commercial Road would be to the left; St Peter's Court, not far from the High Street, is visible between the two cranes on the left. Today, the Tom Crisp Way roundabout is where the photographer once stood. Unofficially named by local residents as the Maconochie roundabout, being the nearest to the old Maconochie-CWS factory site in Riverside Road, nothing now is left to mark the fact that until the 1980s almost three-quarters of the town's estimated working population of 19,000 were once employed in this one area alone. *(Ken Carsey)*

Tesco's Gunton, Yarmouth Road, 1995. Tesco opened their first Lowestoft out-of-town supermarket in 1995, creating a new route, Leisure Way, which led to Pleasurewood Hills theme park. There were problems from the start: the site was teeming with wildlife, notably the protected great crested newts. Close by rare wild orchids unique to Gunton could also be found. *(Author)*

The northern end of Peto Way, October 1995. Looking towards the outskirts of Oulton village, Peto Way linked Denmark Road to Oulton Road. It had been originally planned as a dual carriageway and to eventually lead onto the A12 to Great Yarmouth. The houses and bungalows to the left are in Oulton village, while in the distance the houses and bungalows on higher ground, mostly on the right, are in Gunton. *(Author)*

Hill Lodge, Yarmouth Road, Gunton, 1995. By now a derelict bungalow, Hill Lodge was originally built at the end of the nineteenth century. It later became a wartime sanctuary for Franciscan priests. Because of its unique, almost Arts and Crafts design, there was some controversy as to its future. All in vain, however, and it became the site of the Potter's Kiln public house and motel car park. *(Author)*

The First and Last public house and shops on the junction of Crown Street West and Thurston Road, 1995. Crown Street West is on the right and still contains houses linked to the Lowestoft China Factory. P.W. Griggs ran a grocery store here in 1968; however, in 1978 the opening of Jubilee Way cut Crown Street in two. The First and Last, on the left, although much rebuilt over the years, retained some vestiges of its antiquity. *(Author)*

Left: The late Jack Rose (left) with town crier David Bullock, Sparrow's Nest Gardens, May 1995. It was the dream of historian Jack Rose to have a museum solely dedicated to those stationed in the town, civil and military, men and women, who died during the Second World War. The Lowestoft War Memorial Museum opened on the fiftieth anniversary of VE Day. It is unique in having its own dedicated memorial chapel. *(Author)*

Below: Jack Rose, Jane Jarvis and John Stannard, 1995. Plans were also afoot to create an independent Heritage Centre following Lowestoft Civic Society's acquisition of the old Wilde's School (seen here in the background) off the High Street. Jack was a 'beacon' in more ways than one. In the driver's seat is the late Jane Jarvis, chair of the Lowestoft Civic Society, while to her right is John Stannard, also of the Lowestoft Civic Society. *(Mick Howes)*

Jack Rose outside the Lowestoft War Memorial Museum and Chapel, Sparrow's Nest Gardens, April 1996. 'Oi, Robbo! Come you down 'ere!' was his response to my taking his photograph. The block nearest to the camera behind the young tree was built at the start of the war and became part of what eventually was officially designated HMS *Europa*, the home of the Royal Naval Patrol Service affectionately nicknamed Harry Tate's Navy. The window on the first floor is a metal-framed original. During the war the Sparrow's Nest played an important role in defending the nation on the high seas. To ensure it was never targeted, the old thatched house (part of which is shown here behind Jack and the two passers-by) lost its roof and its bow windows were hidden. The Sparrow's Nest Gardens and in particular the buildings seen here are now considered an important national monument and a reminder of those men and women who lived or were stationed in Lowestoft and who died during the war. Today, the museum covers both the First and Second World Wars, as well as more recent conflicts, and as such also plays host to visitors whose parents or grandparents were stationed at Lowestoft from 1939 to 1945. The War Memorial Museum can also be justly considered as a memorial in its own right to Jack Rose, who also earned the title 'Mr Lowestoft'. Jack Rose died in February 2000. *(Author)*

London Road South near the busy corner of Carlton Road still had some vestige of its old self; the double shopfront of the South Lowestoft Newsagents, Clayton's Shoes at no. 297, Curiosity Capers and Waveney Tool Hire sat among boarding houses and flats, some of which were being cleaned up and brought back to their Victorian elegance. But this is July 1996 – near the height of the town's summer season and only three people are about. *(Author)*

In May 1997 Lowestoft railway station celebrated the 150th anniversary of the arrival of the railway at the port. Brought to the town by Samuel Morton Peto in 1847, the anniversary celebration was organised by the Jack Rose Old Lowestoft Society in conjunction with the LRN 150 project. Here, well-wishers and railway fans wait for the special Norwich to Lowestoft train to arrive. *(Author)*

The Lord Nelson public house on the corner of Victoria Road (to the left) and Waveney Drive (to the right), seen here from the junction of Kirkley Run. It was built in 1903 and served the men working on the southern shore of Lake Lothing. Trade declined with the loss of Brooke Marine and CWS. In this picture from the 1980s we can see it has been converted to flats. It was demolished in late 1996 and a terrace of modern houses is now on the site. *(Attributed to Ken Carsey)*

The Clapham Arms on the corner of Bevan Street East and Clapham Road, September 1996. Better known as the Clapham Hotel, Explorator employees used to hold their children's Christmas parties on the first floor here in the early 1950s. In the 1960s and early '70s the Lowestoft Philatelic Society also held their meetings here. In 2006 it changed usage from a public house and became Coes. *(Author)*

One of the largest peacetime fires broke out on the night of 31 January and 1 February 1999 at the Hippodrome Bingo Hall in Battery Green Road. Twenty tenders from across Suffolk and Norfolk spent the night controlling the fire, which was eventually limited to the Hippodrome itself with only slight damage to neighbouring properties. Tenders were still standing by at the scene on Tuesday 2 February. *(Author)*

The demolition of the Hippodrome Bingo Hall, Battery Green Road, following the fire. Just how close this fire came to being a major disaster is seen here with the Ananas & Dansk shop next door based in the old Gourock Rope Company premises, and the double-fronted shop on the corner of Suffolk Road. Although the Salvation Army building received little damage Ananas & Dansk, on the other hand, suffered quite a lot, notably to its roof. The alleyway at the rear of the Hippodrome was quite narrow, giving concerns that the fire might easily spread to neighbouring premises in both Suffolk Road and Beach Road. *(Author)*

Opposite: Once the fire was under control and the building declared safe, the job of demolition began in earnest. The interior had been completely destroyed. This photograph was taken on 5 February 1999 (it was only then that photographers were allowed this close to the scene), and even then, the ruin was still smouldering. The roof of the Salvation Army citadel next door shows how close it came to destruction. The box-like structure in the distance is the Somerfield multi-storey car park. *(Author)*

Above: London Road North, summer 1999. This was Lowestoft town centre in the final months of the twentieth century. BHS is on the immediate left and we also see the premises of Stead & Simpson, Specsavers and Timpson. Woolworths (centre right) was still with us. The clock in the distance was where everyone gathered to welcome the new Millennium. (*Author*)

Left: Regretfully, in 1999 we lost the much-respected journalist and writer Trevor Westgate. Seen here in front of Wilde's Old School in late 1995 with Lowestoft Civic Society's Jane Jarvis, Trevor did much to promote the town's heritage and history through his column in the *Lowestoft Journal*. He died tragically at his home in March. Jane died in November 2011, and is also remembered as a great supporter of the town's heritage. (*Mick Howes*)

The North Quay Retail Park, June 1999. Opened on the site of Eastern Coachworks, several town centre shops moved into what was the first retail park of its kind in Lowestoft. From left to right are Homestyle, Halfords (which moved from London Road North), Lidl (later to move across the road) and Currys – which also moved from London Road North. For a short while a bus service was tried out which also travelled via Norwich Road. *(Author)*

Tesco, London Road North, June 1999. Taxis shared this part of the town centre with the buses. Although Norfolk & Suffolk Finance has gone, both Tesco and Lowestoft Electrical are still with us. Tesco arrived in Lowestoft in 1964 on the site of Curtiss' Restaurant, noted in the 1950s for its large banner which hung over the pavement. *(Author)*

Above: Dedication of the Trevor Westgate Memorial Rose Garden, Sparrow's Nest Gardens, August 1999. From left to right: Malcolm Berridge, chief executive of Waveney District Council; Maureen Mellor; Jack Rose; Cherry and Michael Westgate. The dedication was led by WDC's chairman, Cllr John Taylor. Guests included Bob Blizzard MP, and *Lowestoft Journal* editor Barry Hartley. *(Author)*

Left: Billy Hansford in action filming in the High Street, July 1999. The brother of Brooke Marine historian Peter Hansford, Billy was an eccentric character, especially as he grew older. His love of photography went hand in hand with his London Marathon running. Billy lived until his eighties and died in June 2010. He is seen here standing in front of no. 85 High Street, built after the Second World War for Lowestoft Co-op and now an Indian restaurant. *(Author)*

Westgate Department Stores, London Road North, looking south towards Lowestoft Electrical and the bus stop outside Tesco. Since late 2011, Westgate's changed its name to Beales. It was on this site that in 1945 Lowestoft planned to have a civic centre and town hall with a design based on Norwich's city hall. *(Author)*

London Road North, 1999. Concluding the town centre in those final months of the twentieth century, we return to what was once, fifty years earlier, a derelict bomb-site. Most of the shops here were rebuilt between 1951 and the late 1950s. H. Samuel was soon to lose its famous clock following refurbishment a year later. The two-storey row of shops near the camera was built in 1951 and included the site of Waller's Restaurant, destroyed in January 1942 and where many of the 70 people died in the raid. *(Author)*

Mutford Lock and Bridge, Oulton Broad, seen here in May 2000, proves how well a properly designed crossing should work. Traffic now bypassed the village centre which remains the gateway to some of the best scenery the Norfolk Broads has to offer. However, the overall traffic dilemma continues with additional vehicles crossing at Oulton Broad to avoid the Bascule Bridge in the centre of town. Although there are roundabouts on each side as you approach Mutford Bridge, additional problems are caused at the railway crossings – one in Victoria Road and the crossing at Oulton Broad North which serves the busy Lowestoft to Norwich line. The smaller of the two traffic roundabouts, the one on the Oulton side of Bridge Road, can be seen behind the pedestrian on the right walking towards the camera. Hayden's the chemist had the shop immediately behind the roundabout. The Wherry Hotel is on the extreme left. *(Author)*

5

THE MILLENNIUM & BEYOND

LT1005 *St Antony*, new in 1999 and seen here in 2000 moored in the Trawl Dock, was the last trawler to be designed for the Lowestoft fishing industry. Owned by Colne Shipping, whose once-great fleet was now down to six boats, two years later, in 2002, the last Lowestoft trawler, LT88 *St John*, was laid up – a victim of EU red tape. In October that same year, *St Antony* was reported to be in Dutch hands. *(Author)*

Sanyo TV factory, School Road, 2000. Sanyo came to Lowestoft in 1982 shortly after the closure of the Philips factory. The company had been attracted to the old Pye/Philips site by the skill of the workforce. Although a Japanese company, it survived into the new millennium to become the last television receiver manufacturer in Britain. The rapid development of flat-screen technology, however, saw the factory close in February 2009. *(Author)*

The Claremont Pier undergoing cleaning for the forthcoming summer season, 2000. In an attempt to revitalise the resort, Kirkley went through a complete and impressive revamp. The Claremont Pier, now looking its best, was approached via an avenue of specially designed lamp standards. Wellington Terrace Gardens, on the left, added to the splendour, and the car park behind the hedge on the right was also improved. *(Author)*

Chadds department store in London Road North did itself proud in that first year of the millennium. The most impressive façade of the store – the double-bay windows – opened in 1902 as Flood's stationers and printers. It later became the Coronet cinema and in the early 1920s was renamed the Theatre de Luxe. Chadds began at nos 70 and 72 London Road North, today's main entrance. Following a distinguished war service, George Victor Nudd Chadd took over from his father, eventually expanding the store to the size we see in the photograph. Colonel George Chadd as he was known, died in June 1997 aged eighty-nine. Until controlling interest was sold to Palmers in 2004, each summer the whole front of the store would be covered in flowers; quite a comparison with the red-brick block on the left belonging to Boots. To the right is Johnsons the dry cleaners, which also cut keys. Next to this is Hughes, a local company that has expanded over the years to cover much of Norfolk and Suffolk. *(Author)*

The Britten Centre market opened in 1988 and is seen here in April 2000. It originally followed the tradition of stalls under canvas which were taken down when not in use. In the background to the left is QD, while on the right, along the passage to Clapham Road is Lowestoft Library, which opened in 1975. The Britten Centre arcade was opened in 1987, marking the final part of the town's post-war reconstruction. The present stalls were erected in 2005. *(Author)*

Hotdog stand, London Road North, taken from the corner of Beach Road in summer 2000. As these young girls confirm, it did a roaring trade in an area of the town centre which had a proliferation of small cafés and restaurants. The two boys are walking past the NatWest Bank towards the post office. The stall and the flowerbeds all went in 2005. *(Author)*

The entrance to Lowestoft Fish Market in 2000 looked more like an entrance to a rig repair and construction area. Where the Rossfish office and processing hall once were, cars and vans are now parked. SLP, the builder of the rigs in the background, was the last great engineering company in Lowestoft; however through no fault of its own, it nearly closed when one of its customers went bankrupt. *(Author)*

Christchurch and Whapload Road in that millennium year were now part of the North Denes Industrial Estate. On the left behind the lamp post with the sign to the magistrates' court and the Kawasaki motorcycle showrooms is the new police station, which had opened in June 1979. The older buildings belong to Christchurch and are the only vestiges left of the old Beach community. John Grose car and van showrooms, on the right, were rebuilt in 2011. *(Author)*

Birds Eye Foods offices, Whapload Road, 2005. These and the discount bed centre are separated by Rants Score. Following the demolition of the Eagle Brewery in the 1960s, Birds Eye had a freezer store here. Looking north from Wilde's Street (which also leads to Ness Point, the most easterly point in Britain), Birds Eye processing plants now have most of this side of the Denes. *(Author)*

Woolworths, London Road North, summer 2005. Although people were extremely unhappy about the removal and subsequent disappearance of the clock and the flattening of Queen Elizabeth Place during the precinct's redevelopment, Woolworths soldiered on come what may. It had reopened on its original pre-war site in 1951 following the rebuilding of the store obliterated in May 1941 and became popular with many visiting the town. From what I recall in those early years, the store had a café for a short period. In an era of baby-boomers, what also struck me then as a four-year-old, even as late as 1951 there was an area near the entrance allocated for prams. Well into the 1960s female shop assistants served behind counters selling everything from cosmetics and sweets to records. Remember the Embassy label LPs, EPs, 45s and 78s? Stanley Gibbons stamp packs for 6d encouraged many a youngster to take up philately. Everything changed when the store was refurbished in 1980; self-service arrived and Woolworths became a completely different place to shop. The Waveney Sunrise Scheme Phase Three began in August 2004. Financed mainly by the East of England Development Agency, the planners appeared to ignore what Lowestoft people wanted for their town centre. The arcade of trees went (most then twenty years old) and the seats and raised flowerbeds all disappeared; but the most controversial (apart from the loss of the trees) was the demolition of the clock, by then known as the Princess Di clock but still a focal point for the town to show its alliance and affection for the royal family. In fact, the loss of this clock is a sore point to this day. To add insult to injury, its replacement was a small hanging timepiece outside Sports Direct. *(Author)*

Opposite: Morlings: the House of Music, 149–51 London Road North, August 2006. Morlings was a family-owned business with an international reputation that had been in the town for over a century. The business expanded beyond their musical origins into electronics. In July 2006 Morlings returned to what they were famous for – music and musical instruments – and transferred to Kirkley, to no. 178 London Road South. They eventually closed in June 2012. *(Author)*

Nos 105–7 London Road North, c. 2006. The new pedestrian precinct is nearly finished and replacement trees have been planted. Shoe Zone is on the extreme left; the shop to let was built in the entrance to Gordon Road bus station and is now a charity shop. The interesting shop is QS, which had a part of Woolworths. Woolworths itself is on the extreme right. *(Author)*

Barber Richmore, Riverside Road, c. 2006. What appeared to be a warehouse on the South Quay was all that survived of Barber Richmore following the demolition of the old CWS and Lowestoft Canning factories in the late 1990s. As far as the photographer could see, the building, or at least the site, was empty. To give some idea of its location, behind the building is the silo in Commercial Road. *(Author)*

Royal Plain looking towards Pier Terrace, c. 2005. The Waveney Sunrise Scheme also included the South Lowestoft and Kirkley resort which also meant changing the road system travelling south along Marine Parade. The Bridge House (the old Harbour Hotel) was still open despite all going on around it. In the background are the shops in Pier Terrace. On the extreme left, the art deco bus shelter is being removed. *(Author)*

The Wherry Hotel, Oulton Broad, winter 2007. Seen in a November in weather that almost mirrored the cause of the East Coast floods of 1953, Lowestoft and Oulton Broad were literally millimetres away from the worst floods for over half a century. By a miracle, the wind direction changed, blowing the waves away from the shore. The following morning saw extra high tides. Both the Asda supermarket and the Wherry had narrow escapes. *(Author)*

The last day of Woolworths, 6 January 2009. In 2008, the company announced the unthinkable: all their branches in Britain were to close. Many of the smaller branches closed that same year, but Lowestoft was one of the most successful and stayed open until the final day of trading. Its closure created a large hole in the life of the town. *(Author)*

Everything was being sold that final day; from remaining retail stock to the store's fixtures and fittings. Many were bought purely as souvenirs and only a few items were left. While the last customers and well-wishers came in one door, at the back, shelves and general fittings were being packed up for prospective buyers. *(Author)*

QD Stores, London Road North, 2011. Although it took some time to confirm a buyer, by the end of 2010 QD, who already had a branch in the Britten Centre, eventually opened a second branch in the old Woolworths store. During the summer of 2011 it became the backdrop for a trailer offering free information on the changes in terrestrial digital television. Woolworths may have gone, but the building looked as impressive as ever. *(Author)*

Surrey Street, looking east towards Beach Road and the cranes of SLP, 2009. A failed creditor caused problems for SLP and for a time it seemed that yet one more important employer would have to close down, fortunately a buyer came forward and oil and gas rigs and their maintenance still continue on the site today. NatWest Bank is on the corner on the right. *(Author)*

Local authority offices, Marina, May 2009. This building, constructed on the site of the Great Grimsby Coal, Salt and Tanning Company's premises, was originally opened as the town's job centre, located close to the old Labour Exchange. Following the job centre's move to Rishton House in Clapham Road, Waveney District Council took it over as its town centre office. The Marina Theatre is on the right. *(Author)*

The Royal Philharmonic Orchestra has been Lowestoft's resident orchestra since 2005, continuing a rich heritage that goes back to the nineteenth century of famous orchestras and performers visiting the town. In 2011, when this photograph was taken, the Royal Philharmonic was in its sixth year at Lowestoft, playing at the Marina Theatre, their home when in the town. *(Author)*

Above: Jarrolds, Beach Road, March 2011. Built in the 1890s as Floods' printing works, this corner premises became Jarrolds office equipment centre in the 1970s. After the closure of Jarrolds town centre shop in January 1997, the Beach Road shop also took over the arts and stationery side. Like other town centre shops, it suffered badly from 2007 to 2010 when not only was the town centre undergoing repairs, the Bascule Bridge area was as well. It closed at the end of March 2011. *(Author)*

Right: Iron support, Jarrolds, Beach Road. Much of Victorian Lowestoft was built by local industry. In the days before J.W. Brooke made a name for himself as a shipbuilder, he supplied the town with railings, drain covers, shop fronts and, as here, iron frame supports for Floods. Erected in the early 1890s, these were still in place on the Grove Road side of the shop in 2011. *(Author)*

History can also be discovered purely by accident, as in the case of the Tesco expansion of its Gunton supermarket in 2006 which also involved enlarging its car park. The relocation of the Tesco filling station to the opposite side of Leisure Way also revealed a substantial source of grey clay and chalk boulders which may have been part of the clay vein that would have supplied an early brickworks nearby and may also have supplied Phillip Walker, the joint founder of the Lowestoft China Factory which opened in 1760. Once part of the Gunton Old Hall Estate of Hewlin Luson and from 1764 owned by Sir Charles Saunders, there are still clay pits and clay pit infills in the Gunton area to this day. Looking east beyond the Tesco car park is another possible source of clay used in brickmaking. It was on this latter site that the habitat of the great crested newt was discovered in the 1990s. *(Author)*

Major road resurfacing in Hollingsworth Road in August 2009 revealed part of the original concrete slab road system laid down by young German prisoners of war in late 1945. Looking towards Yarmouth Road, with Harry Chamberlain Court on the extreme left, and with Europa Road hidden behind the large hedge at the rear of the white van on the right, the old road appeared generally to be in as good condition in 2009 as it was in 1945. Harry Chamberlain Court was built in the late 1980s around the notorious Telesia Court flats, following the deaths of two members of a family in a fire in late July 1985. Telesia Court itself was built in 1964 on the site of some of the estate's prefabs, demolished in 1963. Returning to the right-hand side of the road, these houses were built as part of the initial phase of the town's reconstruction following its devastation in the Second World War. Begun in 1946, the severe winter of early 1947 has left its mark on the brickwork on the end house nearest the camera. The roadworks were finished in October 2009; most of the concrete slabs are still in place today. *(Author)*

Above: Bob Blizzard, MP for Waveney, opening The Yard project, Roman Hill, *c.* 2009. Labour MP for Waveney from 1997 to 2010, Bob succeeded the Conservative candidate David Porter at the 1997 General Election. The Yard project was one of those supported by Lowestoft Together, a government-sponsored scheme led mainly by residents of the town's nine deprived wards, between 2006 and 2009. *(Author)*

Left: The British runner Paul Evans opened the first summer event at the newly founded Gunton Community Park in 2004. Paul had just made his mark as an international sportsman and naturally he was the main attraction for young would-be sportsmen and women. Lowestoft retains a good reputation in competition sports of all types; in recent years, Kirkley, for example, has seen the rise of Anthony Ogogo as a successful young international boxer. *(Author)*

The Revd Colin Napper, minister of Gunton Baptist Church, retired in September 2010 after 31 years. He was one of the longest-servicing church ministers in Lowestoft since the nineteenth century. Both he and his wife Jan did much to help his community through the traumatic years of the late 1990s and with community leader Ann Hubbard, laid down the foundations for today's pioneering Gunton Estate community hub. *(Author)*

Mayor and mayoress of Lowestoft Malcolm and Yvonne Cherry enjoying their day at the first grass-raking at Gunton Community Park, August 2009. Lowestoft's mayors were reintroduced at the start of the new millennium but unlike their predecessors, today's mayoral position is that of a representative at functions and events. Nevertheless, it is still an honour much prized and not taken lightly. *(Author)*

Town Hall, High Street, winter 2005. Increasing traffic caused the town's buses many problems, especially the Gunton 101 and 107 services. Larger buses were needed to bring passengers into the town, but as seen here on the right, they had problems getting past the two vans as well as vehicles parked on the other side. Eventually the two services had to be withdrawn. Trade in the High Street suffered accordingly. *(Author)*

Queuing to cross the Bascule Bridge, Jubilee Way, 2011. Lowestoft's third crossing has yet to happen, just as there is no sign of the present bridge becoming a four-lane bridge. The flats on the right are constructed on the site of part of the old medieval town. Jubilee Way itself was officially opened in 1978 to mark the Silver Jubilee of Her Majesty the Queen the previous year. *(Author)*

Waiting to cross the Bascule Bridge, summer 2011. Travelling south past Belle Vue Park, Sparrow's Nest Gardens and the almost hidden High Light, the car on the right is waiting to come out of Park Road. *(Author)*

Not all the problems are on the north side of the Bascule Bridge, of course; this is Belvedere Road outside Asda, with traffic almost gridlocked waiting to cross to the town centre. Part of the Waveney Sunrise project, for drivers it has proven a disaster. Although taken in July 2009, the situation here has not changed. The dual carriageway from here to Pier Terrace is one of the most dangerous roads in the town. Beyond the cars on the left are three workshops which have never been used since they were built. *(Author)*

Three of Lowestoft's notable heritage authors with Ray Whitehand, one of Suffolk's many intrepid writers on local village history, Waterstones, 2007. Literature and the arts are endemic in a town that has been host to authors and men of letters in the past such as Charles Dickens (who stayed at Somerleyton Hall), Edward Fitzgerald, George Borrow and Joseph Conrad (who was introduced to the English language here), as well as a plethora of modern writers who occasionally travel up from Southwold and Walberswick, not to mention artists of the calibre of Michael Foreman, Jeffery Camp and, of an earlier era, Edward Seago. Photographed at an impromptu meeting at Waterstones, left to right are: Malcolm White, author of many books on Lowestoft's fishing and railway heritage; Ray Whitehand, who was promoting his new book *At the Overseer's Door*; Ivan Bunn, researcher extraordinaire, who with his American college Professor Gilbert Geiss wrote the definitive book in 1997 on the Lowestoft witch trials of 1662 and proved beyond doubt Lowestoft's close link to the Witch Trials at Salem, New England, thirty years later in 1692; and, of course, yours truly trying to hide the fact I have to use a crutch. Almost all of today's writers on the town of Lowestoft owe a debt in one form or another to one man, the late Jack Rose, considered by many – including myself – as the father of modern Lowestoft history. *(Alison Lund)*

Seagulls gathering around the offal truck, Lowestoft Fish Market, late 1970s. Although we have all had to change our ways and habits and have had to seek new ways to bring employment to the town, the community that really suffered the most was the town's seagulls, who, for over a thousand years, if not more, lived off the remains of fish landed at Lowestoft, firstly in the open on the Denes from before the thirteenth century until the nineteenth; then developing quite vicious techniques purloining whole chunks of fish during the bitterly cold weather up until the time the Waveney Market became enclosed in 1987. Even then, a few daring feathered souls succeeded in procuring a decent meal. Firstly their habitats were demolished, such as the Pier Pavilion and the market itself, until today, in the Queen's Diamond Jubilee year, Lowestoft's seagulls have to fight with the town's pigeons for food, and at one time it seemed they would surely succeed. Even today, more than a few visitors have sat outside a café about to enjoy a fresh cream cake or a sausage roll, only to have an adult gull swoop gracefully down and carry it off from under their noses! The photograph was taken looking towards to the Lowestoft Ice Company's factory. The houses in the background on the left are in Battery Green Road. The Rolls-Royce between the two lorries, as far as I recall, belonged to a member of the Cole family. *(Ernest Graystone)*

ACKNOWLEDGEMENTS

Firstly, may I thank all of my readers who over the years suggested I write a book covering the town's more recent past. Although I agreed to write this book in 2009, it eventually took three years to put together. During that time not only did we lose Woolworths, Chadds, Jarrolds and in recent months Morlings, but physically the town itself has undergone a considerable change.

Among those friends and colleagues who helped me and who regretfully are no longer with us, and who passed away while this book was being written was Ken Carsey, and it is special thanks to his widow, Anne, for allowing me access to much of Ken's photography.

But many are still with us – and thanks once again to Pam Graystone who, as in the past, has kindly given me permission to use her father's photographs. Thanks too to Mick Howes for the use of the photographs of Jane Jarvis taken outside the Old School House in Wilde's Score in 1995. Thanks to bus aficionados David Mackley and Kenny Harper; to Paul and Val Allison; Ann Hubbard of the Gunton Estate Community Hall; the Revd Colin and Jan Napper; Mark Butcher; the late Jack Rose (who donated many prints over the years to my archive); members past and present of the Jack Rose Old Lowestoft Society; Alison Lund; John Stannard and Terry Lynes of the Lowestoft Heritage Workshop Centre; historian Ivan Bunn and to Ruth, Bill, Brenda, Emma, Kelly and the staff at the Suffolk Record Office, Lowestoft. Many thanks also to Kate Chantry of the Suffolk Record Office, Ipswich; Richard and Pat Morling; and to David and Ann Bullard.

Special thanks go to Martin, Howard, Rosie, Belinda, Jackie, David and staff of Jarrolds Ltd, Beach Road, Lowestoft, who over the years supplied me with paper, inks, word-processors, photocopiers, pens and advice. This Lowestoft branch of a long-established business closed in March 2011 after over a century of service. This is my way of saying a special thank you to everyone behind the counter who assisted me over the years and who had been kindness and patience itself in dealing with an eccentric artist-cum-author!

All other material comes from my archive, therefore as always I offer a final debt of gratitude to all those photographers, amateur and professional, known and unknown, without whom this book could not be written.